EYES
FORWARD
Messages
for Today
from Yesterday

EYES
FORWARD
Messages
for Today
from Yesterday

Robert Whitfield Miles, D.D.

SUNSTONE
PRESS

The church in which these sermons were preached was designed and built by Cincinnatus Shryock, well-known architect of the period, in 1872. The picture on the cover and the graphic heading before each sermon depict two enduring Gothic Christian symbols, the tower and the spire, both silent witnesses pointing to the heavens.

© 2000 by Robert Whitfield Miles, D.D.
ALL RIGHTS RESERVED.

Printed and bound in the United States of America. No part of this book may be reproduced in any form or by any electronic or mechanical means including information storage and retrieval systems, without permission in writing from the publisher, except by a reviewer who may quote brief passages in a review.

Sunstone books may be purchased for educational, business, or sales promotional use. For information please write: Special Markets Department, Sunstone Press, P.O. Box 2321, Santa Fe, New Mexico 87504-2321.

FIRST EDITION

Library of Congress Cataloging-in-Publication Data:
Miles, Robert Whitfield, 1890–1952.
    Eyes forward: messages for today from yesterday / Robert Whitfield Miles. —1st ed.
        p. cm.
    ISBN: 0-86534-296-2
    I. Presbyterian Church Sermons. 2. Sermons, American.
I.Title. BX9178. M47E94   1999
252′ .051—dc21   99-38113
                           CIP

Published by SUNSTONE PRESS
      Post Office Box 2321
      Santa Fe, NM 87504-2321 / USA
      (505) 988-4418 / *orders only* (800) 243-5644
      FAX (505) 988-1025
      www.sunstonepress.com

CONTENTS

Introduction / **9**

Eyes Forward / **13**

I Believe in the Holy Ghost / **21**

Mature Minds / **28**

More Strong Meat / **36**

Professed Religion / **46**

The Twenty-Third Psalm / **55**

Search After Truth / **65**

Gallant and High Hearted Happiness / **73**

Ordinary People with Extraordinary Goals / **81**

The Paths of Peace / **88**

The Most Startling Paradox / **95**

Christian Experience Through the Centuries / **104**

The Key to a Better World / **114**

A Prayer of Discovery / **123**

Spiritual Procrastination / **131**

Testing Grounds / **139**

Christianity According to Paul / **146**

A Bulwark Never Failing / **155**

The Might of a Minority / **162**

The Individual Equation / **171**

Christmas Before Christ / **181**

A Peak in Darien / **189**

An Age Old Question / **197**

Rebuilding Ruined Cities / **206**

Greatest Saying of the Old Testament / **213**

Robert Whitfield Miles, D.D.

INTRODUCTION

The reason for publishing this volume of sermons is a personal one: to preserve and pass on what we have of our father's work before it is lost. We have many sermons from a ministry spanning thirty-four years. Their content seems as relevant today as when they were preached from the pulpit of the First Presbyterian Church in Lexington, Kentucky roughly fifty years ago.

Robert Whitfield Miles was born in Richmond, Virginia on October 5, 1890. Educated at Davidson College in North Carolina and Union Theological Seminary in Richmond, Virginia, his formal ministry began in 1917. A disability sustained in college, two world wars, the great depression, and the Korean Conflict formed the turbulent physical and social context of his life.

During the First World War, he served as a YMCA secretary with U.S. troops in the states and in France, a post similar to that of chaplain. In 1920, he became assistant pastor to the First Presbyterian Church of Greensboro, North Carolina. From 1921 until his death in 1952 he served as pastor to three other congregations in the Presbyterian Church, United States: the First Presbyterian Church of Auburn, Alabama, 1921-1925; the Westminster Presbyterian Church in Lynchburg, Virginia, 1926-1933; and the First Presbyterian Church in Lexington, Kentucky from 1933 to 1952. It was during this last pastorate that he began to record his sermons as a participant in radio ministry with other clergy in Lexington.

Robert W. Miles received an honorary Doctor of Divinity degree in 1930 from Washington and Lee University. But Dr. Miles was a scholar in his own right, and in 1939 he published *That Frenchman John Calvin* which anticipated by many years present-day scholarship on Calvin. Also, after its publication in 1944, his work *Christian Reconstruction* was used extensively throughout the Presbyterian Church, United States. This was fitting, because one of his abiding preoccupations had always been to help effect union between the Northern and Southern Presbyterian Churches. Another lifelong effort of his was to foster ecumenism. Thus it was on July 7, 1951 as a "token of gratitude and esteem" the Lexington, Kentucky Chapter of the National Conference of Christians and Jews cited Dr. Miles for his service "to the cause of justice, amity, understanding, and good will among the people of diverse backgrounds in Lexington."

This scholarship and these concerns are, we believe, reflected in many of the sermons in this volume. We believe also that they express his faith in a loving and forgiving God revealed through the life and ministry of Jesus Christ, and demonstrate his capacity to love all people. This capacity was far-reaching. He viewed the human condition with tolerance, and he ministered to people with understanding and compassion. At the same time, he exhorted his congregations to build the kingdom of heaven on earth: in their city, their government, their families, their places of work. With a directness that unsettled and challenged he preached with righteous indignation against racial and religious bigotry, grinding poverty, ignorance, and greed. Loving God meant loving and ministering to those around us; in fact, that was how God would know we loved Him. There was no substitute.

The sermons' common theme is that God's purposes for human beings have grown steadily clearer throughout history. He preached with optimism and hope for the ultimate triumph of God's purpose over evil. It is in this basic way that the sermons offer a compelling antidote to the dangers of fanaticism, exclusion, and religious bigotry which characterize much of the spiritual landscape in the world today: tel-evangelism's greed and hypocrisy, the hatred and destructiveness of apocalyptic sects, the horror of religious and ethnic wars in eastern Europe, in the middle and far east.

We have chosen twenty-five of the recorded sermons which we believe are representative of his preaching. Included among them are some from his goal to preach from all books of the Bible in sequence. The onset of what became his final illness interrupted this series at the book of Micah, when he died on January 8, 1952.

Robert W. Miles, Jr.
Marian Miles Morris-Zepp
Edward W. Miles

EYES FORWARD

Undated

Philippians 3: 13-14 "... forgetting those things which are behind, and reaching forth unto those things which are before, I press toward the mark for the prize of the high calling of God in Christ Jesus."

This is one of the sayings of Paul that attracts attention at once and stimulates your imagination. It is well to remember when it was written. Paul was a man past 60, who was held in a Roman prison, probably in Rome, though some think it was Ephesus; and while held in detention was writing to his friends in the church at Philippi. This church, which had been organized in the home of Lydia, a businesswoman in that city, was the first Christian organization on what we now call the continent of Europe. Philippi was a Roman colony settled by the veterans of the imperial legions; so that we know it was a community of hardy folk, knit into an active city. From all internal evidence in this letter, we realize that Paul felt most kindly toward them, for the whole epistle breathes optimism and appreciation. There is no book in the New Testament which has a more joyous note than this short letter to the church at Philippi.

This is worth mentioning, for the author was old beyond his years, having lived a strenuous life many centuries before that term originated. One would think that he would dwell upon the past, but that is not the case. This verse, as you see, contains two words: "forgetting" and "pressing." As we examine it, we shall see more clearly how his face was always to the front and that he was interested not so much in what had gone before as what was yet to be accomplished. As these two words are the key to the statement, let us examine them in order.

This word "forgetting" may be misleading. One does not forget completely. In fact, it is often necessary to remember what has gone before in order to live and act in the present and future. However, memory should not be a dwelling-place but rather it should be, to use a modern expression, the propulsion pit for new life.

One of the most beautiful poems that Tennyson wrote is called "Ulysses." He pictures the old king Ulysses returning to his home after the ten years of the Trojan War and the ten subsequent ones when he wandered over all the Mediterranean area. His son Telemachus was reigning. All was moving smoothly and the old king, mighty warrior and statesman that he was, felt that he could not settle down in his island abode. His war craft was ready, the rowers were at the oars and Ulysses expresses his philosophy of life before he leaves for the last time the scenes of his youth and early manhood. The first sentence that I would remind you of in the poem is this: "I am a part of all that I have met." That is true of each of us. Every experience in life — my heredity and my environment — enters into making *me* as of this moment. One does not escape his past. The countless thoughts, actions and currents that have played upon us enter into making us as of this moment. I am a part of all that I have met, is true in the case of every person in the world.

14

However, while I have gained momentum by the past, today must be judged in the light of today's accomplishments. It is not what my ancestors have done but what I am accomplishing now. It is a splendid thing to have a fine heritage. Men and women before us in the generations who have led upright lives, who have been people of integrity, who have contributed much to society and have worked for the promotion of the Kingdom of God — fortunate the person who has such a background. We recognize, however, that this is not only an asset but a liability. One should be very careful in speaking of the deeds of his ancestors, lest the comparison of his own life should be embarrassing. Where much has been given, much is expected; and a splendid past demands a splendid present. One notices all too often that the descendants of great people fall far short of their famous forebears because they have been content to bask in reflected glory and not to achieve for themselves.

Not only can I not rest today on what my predecessors have done; I cannot rest on what I have done myself. This morning I am not preaching this sermon on last week's effort. This homily must have been prepared and preached on its own merit. Of course one gains skill as the days grow into years, yet if we ever pause and look back, resting on our oars, we soon deteriorate. I no longer am a frequent spectator at athletic events, but I still maintain my interest in games. This summer I followed the career of a young man on the Cincinnati team who was putting together a splendid performance in pitching. Each game that he won brought him nearer to the record, but each game was harder than the preceding one because of this fact. Finally, after winning 16 straight he had only three more victories before he would equal the world's record for consecutive wins. However, Blackwell was defeated in his 17th attempt. The 17th game had to be won on its own merit. The preceding 16 did not count in that afternoon's effort. We should remember always this obvious fact: that the present issue must be met as of today and not in the light of yesterday's results.

The same is true of our joys. One cannot re-live his youth or past pleasures. Years ago a novel called *Conrad In Quest of His Youth* in which the middle-aged Conrad, endeavoring to re-live the scenes of 20 years before, finds that the glamour has departed. Dickens pictured the bride who had been deserted at the altar, living for years in her wedding gown surrounded by the remnants of the wedding feast. Such an unhappy scene caricatures but drives home the fact that today we cannot re-live yesterday's pleasures. Anyone returning to his college campus after an absence of many years realizes this truth. Yet men have always said, "The former days were better than these"; but as the writer of Ecclesiastes reminds us, in so saying they do not act wisely. Sufficient unto yesterday were the pleasures thereof. But for joy today, the present must take care of itself.

What is true of joy holds also for sorrow. One should not dwell in the house of mourning. Life moves forward always. People fall out of the ranks and others step forward to take their places. Life does not stop for the dead. In the Old Testament we read that when Aaron died, the children of Israel mourned 40 days and then proceeded on the march. When Moses died, Joshua took over and led them into the Promised Land. As I look out over the congregation week after week, I can see in my mind's eye scores and scores of people who worshipped here and have now gone to their reward. However, the church does not stop its progress. Every one of my predecessors in this pulpit has died except one; yet the ministry of preaching moves on. And when I am only a memory, some other minister will stand in this place. We cherish the thought of the departed. We hold them in tender and loving memory, but we honor them, not by ceasing all activity in our grief, but in living to the fullest the life we have.

One must not be lost in a maze of regrets over his own mistakes. We know that we have erred frequently, yet if we continue in self-recrimination we lose the way when we desire to make amends. The critic has said that Hamlet lost himself in a labyrinth of thought. All too often we lose ourselves in dwelling on what might have been. At this point modern psychology helps us. It tells us not to detour our unangelic nature but to bring the dark and uncomfortable aspects of our inner lives to the surface. Everyone has evil thoughts, but do not brood on these or feel that they will destroy you. Apply a mature mind to the problem that arose in immaturity. Here proper counseling helps one, and it need not always be professional counseling. The friend that sticketh closer than a brother sometimes gives invaluable assistance.

Frequently these repressions and bottling-up of desires without proper outlet — that is, facing and discussing them — cause people to become zealots and bigots. Many a religious persecutor and zealot has been endeavoring to escape from himself.

Questions of maladjustments in families have caused children to grow up warped and biased. When we realize this, trace them back to their source, we can correct the problem as it exists in the present. In such instances we remember in order to forget.

The above paragraph brings us to Paul's positive admonition. He pressed forward, forgetting the things that were before. He was one who knew how to remember in order to forget. Again Tennyson's Ulysses has a word for this:

> Yet all experience is an arch wherethro'
> Gleams that untravelled world, whose margin fades
> For ever and for ever when I move.

Life should always be before us. We view it from the arch of our experience. We move ever toward the horizon which in turn constantly recedes and beckons us on throughout the days.

Paul was looking forward. He knew that he had killed innocent men, women and children through his religious bigotry. Augustine said long ago that Stephen prayed and Paul was converted. Undoubtedly he never effaced that scene from his memory: the saintly Stephen dying in his own blood on the ground, calling to Jesus Christ, his Savior. That memory only nerved Paul to move forward.

He was also a man who had had great joy and much personal sorrow. He was rich in friends. He had seen the reward of his labors. He had the satisfaction of building deep and wide, yet he did not dwell in these memories.

Paul also had had much personal sorrow. From internal evidence all through The Acts and his letters, we believe that he had been cast off by his family. He had seen his friends die. He had had indignities heaped upon him. As mentioned above, he was at this time in prison. Yet he said, "I press forward."

The words of our Lord come to us at this point: "He who would gain his life must lose it." We lose it in constructive living in His Kingdom. The kind of life that Jesus taught and lived and died for, Paul called the "upward life." You and I speak of this together every week. We realize that we must find inner peace even as Christ and Paul did if we are going to live their kinds of lives. I think perhaps the greatest contribution that Jesus made was his emphasis on, and demonstration of, inner peace. We worship here week by week in order that our souls may be refreshed and our minds ordered as we seek after this peace. We recognize that this is a paradox in life: the acquisition of inner peace while at the same time we maintain constant warfare against wrongs that are without. Only as one presses toward the upward life can he cause this equilibrium of the soul.

One does not have to look far for his opportunities for constructive living. They are right at hand. So often we place our thoughts on the far horizons and forget the immediate environment. We go back into our homes where the key is to worthwhile living. We know that lives are made or marred in the homes. All too often mature people are called upon to salvage their lives because the atmosphere of the home was not conducive to satisfactory development. The first place to press forward in the Christian life is within the family circle. No matter how old we are, we can start today to change our attitudes if we have not been contributing to the peace, tranquility and happiness of our immediate family circle.

The whole church organization provides a medium for constructive living. We move forward through the agency of the church. All of us know that the church is composed of people, but we should never forget its divine origin and head. Imperfect as it is, it is the bride of Christ. I cannot stress too strongly the loyalty we should have toward our church as a channel through which we release our Christian life into the world.

When we think of constructive living , we turn naturally also to our privileges and responsibilities as citizens. There is always a danger that people in this country, that has prospered beyond the fondest dreams of the founding fathers, are apt to dwell upon the glories of the past rather than the needs of the present and the challenges of the future. Mr. Justice Brandeis said once that our independence was won by those who valued liberty both as an end and as a means. They believed liberty to be the secret of happiness and courage to be the secret of liberty. Sometimes we are prone to feel that as individuals we can do little to help shape the policy of our nation in its local and international approaches. Nothing could be more fallacious. You and I are called upon to press forward here, rather than to stumble forward through looking backwards over our shoulders.

I am inspired constantly by my friends who are in their 60s, 70s, 80s and even 90s. Here on my sermon notes I have jotted down the names of some members of the church who come within these age ranges. Of course I shall not name them, and it is not an exhaustive list; yet it heartens me constantly to be associated with people whose eyes are to the front and who do not dwell in the mansions of memory. The other day I dropped in to call on one of our officers, who is now past 90 years of age. I found him engaged in writing an article for a medical journal. Though he has spent a long and useful life, he is still keenly interested in making a contribution to the science of medicine.

The other day I read the memoirs of Dr. Walter Lingle, who is now president emeritus of Davidson College. For the conclusion of his book he dwelt on his position as president emeritus. His study looks out over the college campus where he spent so many fruitful years, but the tone of his writing evidenced the fact that he was not looking backward but still pressing forward in a quiet way through the manifold opportunities that his present position presents. Browning was everlastingly right when he said, "Grow old along with me; the best is yet to be—the last of life for which the first was made." It is always tragic when one has not lived in the early flights of life in such a way that the last ones can carry out this statement.

In closing we turn again to Ulysses. Said he,

> For my purpose holds
> To sail beyond the sunset, and the baths
> Of all the western stars, until I die.

Church tradition says that after Paul was released from prison, he made a journey to the west, preaching as far as Spain. We know that after this letter to the Philippians his contributions to the Christian cause were manifold. In his own life he exemplified that he could *forget* and *press forward* to the upward calling. May we too follow his example.

I BELIEVE IN THE HOLY GHOST

Sunday, June 26, 1949

Today I have chosen for our text the words that we repeat each Sunday in the Apostles' Creed: I believe in the Holy Ghost. As we say the Apostles' Creed week by week, we remind ourselves of those basic principles which the Christian Church has believed throughout the years. We remember that it was a compilation, as it were; that in the Church in Apostolic days on down through the next five centuries, men gradually formulated what they believed; and finally it emerged in the form that we now call the Apostles' Creed, which in its completed and present state dates somewhere around the year 600.

In that Creed, you notice, they emphasize belief in God the Father, in Christ the Son, the Holy Ghost, in the Church and in the communion of saints, and in the fact that there is life everlasting; also the forgiveness of sin. Those words were compiled many years ago. Men's thinking has changed somewhat in basic lines. We do not stand here week by week and repeat it parrotlike and say that each comma and dotting of an i we believe. It is not in the Bible; it is man-made. But it forms a very splendid summary of our belief; it also gives us great symbolic emphases in our belief.

One phase of it then today is my theme, because it is an important phase, yet frequently overlooked. "I believe in the Holy Ghost." You and I call ourselves Trinitarians, in contradistinction to those who call themselves Unitarians. Unitarians believe in God the Creator and Ruler of the universe and the Father of us all. They do not accept the deity of our Lord, nor do they put any emphasis on the Holy Spirit. They are Unitarians; and we call ourselves Trinitarians, because we stress a threefold aspect of God. You hear the phrase or the expression "the Holy Trinity" frequently. There are churches that are called Trinity Church. You and I are Trinitarians, and we have a threefold approach to God.

Now one recognizes at once that it is a very difficult thing to define God, or to experience Him sometimes. But when you begin to capture the conception in words and put it down in a formula, you experience difficulty. Yet one must have beliefs if he is going to have actions. Every once in a while you hear a person say, "Well, I have no creed." That of course is absolutely foolish. Everyone has a creed. They may not have the Apostolic Creed, but they have a creed; for the word "creed" means "belief." You can never act without a belief.

For instance, you may be a salesman. You may sell stocks and bonds, or insurance, or property, anything. That's your activity. You never sell any real estate or any insurance or stocks and bonds if you do not believe in those things. You try to sell me something that you do not believe in , and I detect at once the falseness of your approach, the hollowness of it. One must believe in order to act. Therefore when a person tells you they have no creed, they mean that they do not have this particular creed; but they have a creed—do not worry.

Now in our creed—this particular one—we are talking about God. I remind you that long ago Mohammed said this in the Koran: Say not that God is a third of three. That's a very wholesome admonition. We do not worship three Gods. We worship one God, but we believe that God has at least three manifestations. Now we know that in this world there is order. We do not think that this world just happened. There are physical laws that make it possible. As I hear the drone of the airplane overhead at this moment, as I stand in front of three electronic devices as I speak, one that records what I am saying, one that enables you in the pew to hear if you are deaf, one that enables a person far beyond this room to hear, we have evidence of the application of these laws. Men have thought God's thoughts after Him, until planes can fly in the air and voices can be transferred to the ends of the earth.

If there are these physical laws, you see, if there is design and purpose in the universe, there is intelligence back of it. No order without intelligence. And if there is intelligence back of it, there is personality back of it, for you have personality where you have intelligence. No intelligence devoid of personality. When we speak of God then, we speak of Him not as a body; we speak of Him as an Intelligence, as a Personality — the great Personality of the world. We call Him God, we call Him Father, the Jews called Him Elohim, we have various names; but this Personality, this Spirit, if you will, is the force behind and in the universe.

And that is our general conception of God the Father who loves us, who is the spiritual intelligent Personality back and in and through the world. In the process of the years men had a revelation of God which was different. There came into the world a Man known as Jesus Christ. He made some very startling claims. The most startling was this: that "I and my Father are one;" that "he that hath seen me hath seen the Father." So we say that Christ is God-like, and that God is Christ-like. We need to have visible manifestations, visible symbols of life, and Jesus was the physical visible symbol of God. The Word of God became flesh; it was incarnate in a man, and we know what the character of God is through the character of Christ.

Well, Jesus said this: I am going back to my Father. I shall not remain in this world very long. I will not leave you comfortless. I will send you the Comforter — the Holy Spirit. So when Jesus Christ left this world in the flesh, he said that he would send the Holy Spirit — the third person of the Trinity. So there came into the world the understanding on the part of men of this spirit of God, this spirit of Christ in the world which we call the Third Person in the Trinity. God's Personality in the world — that is what the Holy Ghost or the Holy Spirit is.

Men talk a lot about the second coming of our Lord. He has come already the second time, you see. If he ever comes again in the flesh, it will not be the second coming. It will be a continuing coming. As you know, I personally think he will never come back, in the flesh, because he's here in the spirit. He's already come back. Calvinism stresses the Holy Spirit and not the second physical, visible return of our Lord. But that I assure you is purely an incidental matter. Believe as you care to and as you get your satisfaction.

Now what is this matter of God's personality in the world? What do we believe about it? I spoke of these physical manifestations here with us this morning. Men talk today of energy, that there is no such thing as matter — it's all energy. This pulpit is not solid, but that it's matter in constant motion, energy in constant motion. For practical purposes it is solid, but scientifically it's a form of energy. You are a form of energy and I am a form of energy. Well, what energy? The basic energy of the world. The Hebrews said, "In the beginning God" and "the Spirit of God moved upon the face of the deep" and the earth began to take form. That word that they used is *ruah* — the Spirit of God, that which makes Him.

Now this word "Holy Ghost" is an old English word. We call it Holy Spirit now. The ghost was the breath or the spirit of a man. When they spoke of giving up the ghost they meant dying; and because men spoke of giving up the ghost and dying, then they began to use the word ghost, which was the symbol of life. You gave up the ghost (you died); therefore they used the word ghost to define the spirit of a man that wandered around after his death; and they would say that in a cemetery you would see ghosts. What were ghosts? They were spirits, disembodied spirits that were wandering around. The bodies had given up the ghosts and the ghosts had no place to dwell in the flesh. That is why this expression of "I saw a ghost" comes in. But it is the life—this thing that is ME, that is YOU—and the Spirit of God, this infinite power of God working throughout all time. He created the world through this long evolutionary process that is still going on. He created man through a long evolutionary process. And what makes us a person? Why, it is the spirit of God within me. I am made in the image of God—not in the earthly image of God. God has no body. God is not a man. I have God's spirit in me.

But also the world has God's spirit. It is all a manifestation of divine power, of divine personality . . .the heart of the Creator pulsing in life. Some people used to talk about the earth being the body of God, and they were called pantheists. We are panentheists; we believe that God is *in* everything.

Then you see if we really believe that, we believe that God is here; His Holy Spirit is here. He is here touching us constantly and giving us power to live. One cannot visualize just a spirit. One can look back on Jesus Christ and remember a God-man in the flesh and his teachings and his life. But when he departed, he sent back to us his personality—this power that is in the world, this power of God.

He touches me in my personality, in my conscious mind, in my unconscious mind, in my subconscious mind. If some of my friends and church members are hearing me at this moment in their homes and recognize my voice, they say the voice of Dr. Miles; and they have an idea of the personality of Dr. Miles. But you see God does not speak to me audibly. If my voice can go through the ether, God's spirit certainly can go through life; and His spirit touches my Spirit, my mind and my heart, both consciously and subconsciously. And I open to Him in prayer and He enters and abides.

25

So after all, you see, when I say I believe in the Holy Ghost, I simply mean that I believe that God is here, that He is present in the world, touching you and touching me. He's in this sanctuary, He's in my heart, He's in your heart, He's in the life of the world — God is everywhere. God is, and this is His world.

Now one does not have to be a mystic to believe that. Some people are naturally more mystical than others. You may never have been caught up in a vision, but some people have. You may not be able to have telepathic communications with others, but some people have. No one knows what is back of this apparent world. I do not know and neither do you. I cannot go back in time nor can I go forward at present, but some day I shall be able to . We speak of the fourth dimension as time and the fifth dimension as future life. Well, when we get into the fifth dimension, the future life, it's perfectly possible that we shall have the sixth dimension for coming back into this present life in our thinking. Who knows but what I can commune with those who have gone before? I would not gainsay it. The spirit of God is in all of life . . .in the world today, in the world behind, in the world to come.

When I say I believe in the Holy Ghost, I believe in that which is life and for life and is of the spirit; which is permanent rather than of the flesh, which is transient.

As I close I would remind you of this: that next Sunday morning you and I take part in a ceremony that is a symbol. We call it a "sacrament." And in that sacrament we give voice to just this thing of which I am speaking. In the sacrament of the Lord's Supper we have two elements, bread and wine. Jesus said, "As often as ye eat this bread and drink this wine, ye do show forth the Lord's death until He come." He went on to say, "This is my body broken for you; and this is my blood. . . ." We celebrate his life and his death and his return in the spirit. When the minister prays and sets apart those elements — consecrates them — he says, "to set apart such of these elements as we need for this worship."

There is a branch of the church that believes that when those elements are set aside they actually become the flesh and blood of our Lord; that when a person partakes of that bread, he eats the flesh of God. Of course, my Protestant Calvinistic training would never let me believe that, because my mind would never let me believe it. If one wants to believe it, all right; I have no quarrel with them. But for me, I cannot have intellectual problems like that to hurdle. It just does not gear into my way of living and thinking.

However, we believe that in those elements, Christ is spiritually present. Here he is in the spirit and we go through the symbol of partaking of the spirit within our bodies to strengthen our souls . . .the Holy Ghost, the Holy Spirit, present in the symbols of the sacrament. For always at the Lord's Supper we underscore the belief in the Holy Spirit. We do it every Sunday, but more particularly in the sacrament we have a visible manifestation.

I believe, then, in the Spirit of God — that spirit the author Job mentioned, "There is a spirit in a man and the breath of the Almighty giveth him understanding." And again in Ezekiel at the Valley of the Dry Bones when God said to Ezekiel, "I will put my breath in them. I will put my spirit in them, and they shall live." And every newborn babe, every babe born in Lexington today, or that has ever been born, God says, I will put my spirit in him or in her; and His Spirit enters. That is what differentiates the baby from a mere inanimate object. God's spirit is in me, and I am in God's spirit; and I partake of all of these spiritual values and powers and energies.

I say, then, that I believe in the Holy Ghost; I believe that I am linked by a contact with the only and the ultimate Power in all the universe.

MATURE MINDS

July 31, 1949

The words of our text today are, to me, most interesting; and I trust that through our meditation together, you and I will gain some strength for the days. We do not know who wrote the Epistle to the Hebrews. Formerly men had thought that the Apostle Paul had been the author, but now they feel that he was not the writer but some man who had been trained in the Jewish Law, who had been a faithful follower of Abraham and Moses and then converted to the Christian faith. Whoever he was, he had a rare insight into life, was the master of a polished Greek style, and has been provocative of thought throughout the years.

In the last part of the fifth chapter, he is rather chiding those to whom he wrote because he felt they had relapsed from a mature attitude in life toward a childish one. There is a marked difference between childlikeness and childishness. He felt that they had become rather childish when they should be mature. Consequently, the words with which that chapter finished are the words that I am using today to stimulate our thinking.

Said he to these early Christians, You need milk, not solid food; for anyone who lives on milk is unskilled in the word of righteousness, for he is a child; but solid food is for the mature, for those who have their faculties trained to distinguish good from evil. The King James says "for strong meat belonging to them that are of full age." The modern translations use "maturity" in place of "full age." So if we are mature, we need the solid food of the Gospel; and when we are children, we need the milk of the Gospel.

Now childhood is a very delightful time. It is a period of innocence, trust, sincerity, dreams, anticipations and hope. There are other characteristics of childhood, but those I think remind you. Jesus said, If anyone is going to enter the Kingdom of Heaven, he must become as a little child. However, there is one characteristic of childhood that enters into that more than others. Childhood is the time of hope.

The other day I asked a little girl how old she was. She said, I am four, but I'll soon be five. And any child, that is, a normal child, is thinking not only of the age that he is, or she is; they are always anticipating growing older, growing up. They like to be considered big girls and big boys; and you say to them, That is not the way a big girl would act, the little girl takes firmer hold upon herself because she wants to seem older to you. Childhood is the time of anticipation and of dreams and of hope—looking forward to development.

Now maturity is the time of experience and testing, or when we have been tested, and seasoned. There should be stability in maturity. There should also be hope. I said Jesus said, Except ye become as little children, ye cannot enter the Kingdom of Heaven. Except we have that continuing hope for building a better world within and without, we cannot enter the Kingdom of Heaven.

Nicodemus said to Him, Can a man be born again and re-enter his mother's womb? Jesus answered, "That which is born of the flesh is flesh; but that which is born of the Spirit is spirit." We are continually re-born in the spirit. So one should pray, I think, that on his 50th birthday, for instance, when he awakens, he should have as keen a desire and as lively a hope for the coming days as when he woke on is fifth birthday.

Maturity cannot retard the years. We cannot deal with Time,

29

but we can deal with spirit, and those who enter the Kingdom of Heaven are childlike—in the fact that they have a continuing and renewing hope for the building of God's Kingdom.

Spirit alone, then, is eternal youth. But one would not desire to be a Peter Pan. If you should meet a Peter Pan, you would feel that not only was he an anachronism but that perhaps he had been the invention of an over-sentimental novelist of a day gone by; wonderful novelist as he was. No one wants to be a Peter Pan and never grow up. All of us look forward to the maturing of life with the years.

Now what kind of a life does a mature person have in the field of religion? This constant growth—where has it led? At what point should I view my religion if I am mature? Let me remind you of what we hold as Christianity, this religion of maturity; and as I remind you of it, I mention this fact: that ofttimes people who are mature in many ways are still child-like in their religious conceptions. The great time of loss in Sunday school is between 12 and 15. Many people stop studying the Bible when they are 15, or before. Many of you have not read the New Testament for a long time. I should not like to embarrass you and ask you how long it has been since you read the four Gospels, but the chances are that many of you have not read them of late.

We are mature in the field of business; we think we know something of political movements; we develop this line of thought and that; but there has been a strange block in our religious thinking, and many people never go beyond the intermediate department of the Sunday school in their religious thinking. And many people, even though they have continued to go to Sunday school and church, have never brought a maturity of their minds to bear on religion. They still accept that which was told them as a child and they think of it in child-like terms rather than as mature men and women.

Well, there is a tremendous drama to this thing that we call Christianity. It is the most dramatic study in all the world. I said I would remind you and myself — may I do it? We believe that this world has a God, the Creator and Ruler of this world, who is purposeful in His activity, who knows the end from the beginning, who rules as an intelligent Being. We believe in God.

We believe also as Christians that men have marred the way of God, that we have failed to understand His physical and moral laws; and in the realm of moral law, we have made mistakes. We call those mistakes sin. Last Sunday, you may remember, I mentioned the seven deadly sins the church has enumerated: lust, and anger, sloth, gluttony, covetousness, selfishness or pride, envy or jealously; these sins that are searching and inclusive.

So a mature Christian not only believes in God, but he recognizes sin, both in his own life and in the world. Then comes the greatest drama of it all. A Christian believes that at a given time in history, God entered the life of man in the form of a man, that Jesus Christ came into the world — a God-Man, if you will; Very God of Very God. Also man. Herein is a mystery that we believe, that the plane of God cut the plane of man, and the intersection is the God-Man that we call Jesus Christ; and that if one would know what God is like, study Jesus Christ. What is God like? Like Christ. What is Christ like? Like God. The Christ is God-man. We say that so glibly; we repeat it to ourselves; we pay lip service. But it is the most dramatic conception that man has ever had — that there was in the world a Person named Christ who was Very God of Very God, and yet subject to like temptations as are we.

Then we believe also that this Man who was God, this God who entered into man, suffered; that there is the sorrow of God, that the sin of man killed God; that God died on a cross through the sin of man. And that proved the identification of ourselves with the suffering of God. We are brought nigh unto God and are what we call "saved."

The other day I reviewed a book called *The Meaning of History*, a very profound and a very scholarly book by an author in the East. In his introduction he had these words: "The interpretation of history is, in the last analysis, an attempt to understand the meaning of history as the meaning of suffering by historical action." That the attempt to understand the meaning of history is to understand the meaning of suffering by historical action.

Again you may remember that last week I reminded you that some people think the chief end of man is to have a good time, that pleasure is the be-all and end-all of life; and it isn't. There is no meaning to life unless we enter into the meaning of suffering. And God Himself suffered, and God Himself does suffer, and in Christ as we identify ourselves with the suffering, we begin to understand more of the meaning of life.

Now this, you see, is the religion of a mature person; not a child in the sixth grade; not a person in junior high school—one must develop mentally and spiritually as he takes hold of these facts. For children who are 8 and 10 have known very little of suffering, but who has come to the year of 50 who has not entered into the suffering of mankind?

Said this writer, I am giving you strong meat, solid food. I am not nursing you with a bottle with a nipple on the end of it.

Now the last thing that we hold in this drama is that this God-Man not only was crucified and buried, but that he rose again; that we believe in the continuing life.

Well, there you are, you see. A God who is Creator and Ruler; man, who is imperfect; God, who demonstrates Himself in man, who suffers with and for man, who presented a pattern of life we call the Christian Way; who died, and rose again. If you read that for the first time, you would say, This is the most incomprehensible thing ever written. If you saw it in a movie for the first time, you would say, This is the most dramatic conception ever dreamed. Well, it is the most dramatic. Yet there are in the United States more than half the people who are professedly Christian, many of whom never give it more than a passing thought. But you see we could not stop there, if we do not come a little closer to grips with the meaning of it, for us as mature people.

Where we take hold of it, in our living, is in the life of this God-Man, Christ Jesus . . . the kind of life that He lived and taught; by our standards today, a very strange life, a very impractical one, extremely difficult to follow. Now that word *difficult* is exactly what I mean. It is very difficult to be a Christian. It is tremendously rewarding; it is not easy. If you think it is simple to be a Christian, you are immature in that you have not tried. If in the maturity of your mind you endeavor to do it, with God's help, you recognize at once that it is a hard and arduous undertaking. It is, however, the only hope of the world, the only way of life that will bring to pass, ultimately, the Kingdom of God.

The meaning for me is to understand what I have been speaking of so far, and to live it. It is to accept the challenge of the life of Christ in my own life, to recognize that it is the inwardness of the spirit that makes it possible—not the flesh, but the spirit. Think of this world in which we live—how pagan it is, the tensions, the hatred, the bickering and the strife, the unkindness and the unthoughtfulness, if you will; the anger, and the jealousy; the suspicion that people have. They read into you motives that you do not dream of.

A friend of mine said to me the other day, "You know, I always take people for what they profess. I am accustomed to believing a man, and to accepting him at his statement and his value, but that's not the way most people do." He said, "Most people are trying to read hidden motives and inner meanings. They feel that you are trying to defraud them or to take advantage of them. They wonder what you are up to and there is a feeling of uncertainly in the world." That is all too true. The United Nations assembly; and the American delegates will say one thing and the others will think, I wonder what's back of that? What do they mean? Where is that hidden thought that they will bring out later? You read a legal document and you say, What's in this that I have to watch—that perhaps they will after all slip one over on me? A person is kind to you, and you say, I wonder why they are pleasant? What are they trying to get out of me? What's in it for them? There is an attitude of suspicion on the part of people all too often.

Now I said this is difficult. If we are going to be mature people, we have to recognize that great principle of the worth of the individual in God's sight, and the possibilities of the individual, if you will. And one can reach anywhere for illustrations, but let me just mention one as I close.

Here you and I are now — mature people, theoretically; and I trust we are. We start out this week endeavoring to live the Christian life. We say we are members of the First Presbyterian Church, old, established, respectable group of people who have for the most part more than the average of this world's goods and who live in a pretty pleasant kind of way. Now how are we going to try to live this Christian life? Let me give you one test. Here's one; I could take a dozen, but I'll take this particular one; and between now and next Sunday I'd like you to try it out. Jesus said this: "It hath been said of old, Thou shalt love thy neighbor and hate thine enemies, but I say unto you . . . But *I* say unto you, Love your enemies." "Love your enemies."

Let's stop right there. I trust you have no enemies. It's a very disconcerting thing when you find that you have an enemy; it does something to your personality if you think someone hates you. Suppose, though, that I have an enemy; that you have an enemy; and I am trying to be a mature Christian this week, and Jesus says, Love that enemy. Do you believe that? I mean that's Christianity? Well, it's not my word. I'm just telling you what the Bible says. I'm not the author of the statements of our Lord; I'm just quoting them. You either believe Jesus or you do not. You either say, Well, that's absolutely impossible and I'll just throw it out the window and make no pretense at doing it –or you say, That's a very finespun dream, but Jesus after all was kind of crackpot and no one is going to try to follow that. Or you say, Am I going to try to follow it? I leave it with you. I just make this suggestion: When you are confronted with your enemy that way, at first you want to have an objective view — very difficult to have an objective view in life, but you try to get an objective view. One says to himself, After all, I wonder why he is my enemy? What have I done that makes him my enemy? Perhaps I have been wrong, and I can correct this. Let's examine ourselves and see where I stand, what my position is. And then remember that although he hates you, you recognize he is a child of God — you are not going to hate him. You may not like him. I do not think anywhere in the Bible it says that I must like my enemies. It says I must love them. You know, I do not find everybody equally entertaining, or it's not everybody that I would want to eat a meal with, or take a trip with. Some people bore me, and I know it. And I bore some people, because they have told me. It's just one of those things. But loving them and liking them is a different thing, you see. Loving them in a Christian way, recognizing their worth, being fair to them, not reciprocating hatred with hatred; having an objective view. For that hatred that comes into you will be a cancer in your soul and it will destroy you rather than destroy your enemy.

So Jesus said, It hath been said of old, Thou shalt love thy neighbor and hate thine enemy; but I say into you, Love your enemy. And the beautiful thing is, He demonstrated it; for when His enemies nailed Him on a cross, He said, Father, forgive them; they know not what they do.

I do not know whether you think this is strong meat, but I do; for it is strong meat for me, and I do not eat and digest it easily but with the grace of God I pray daily that I may be an ever-increasingly mature Christian.

MORE STRONG MEAT

August 7, 1949

You will recall that last Sunday morning I meditated with you on the religion of a mature mind, using the words from Hebrews where the writer spoke of milk being for children, but meat for those who are mature. In illustrating one of the features of a mature religion, I quoted the saying of our Lord, "It hath been said of old, thou shalt love thy neighbor and hate thine enemy; but I say unto you, Love your enemies." We saw that if we are going to love our enemies, it is indeed the expression of a mature religious outlook and experience.

Today I would pursue that a little further, using another illustration of our Lord's in this matter of mature religion. I reminded you that Christianity is not a simple matter; it is not easy to be a Christian. It challenges the entire character and the best of a character on the part of any person. Sometimes we are discouraged because Christianity makes such slow progress. Be not discouraged. Minorities always—in the right—go forward. And the reason there are few Christians, comparatively speaking, is that Christianity is very difficult. It runs contrary to human nature. A man's mind and spirit must be made over. If you fail, as all of us do, do not be discouraged, provided you have the outlook and the ideal, and are conscious of the fact that you grow, albeit it may be slowly.

The verse that I am using today as an illustration of mature religion are these words that I read in the latter part of the second Lesson. One verse I have singled out in order that we may focus our attention on that; for all of those verses are cognate to the subject and emphasize what we have in mind. Our Lord was using an illustration from the times when Roman soldiers or couriers bound upon messages and business of the emperor would impress into service anyone that they met and compel him to guide them for at least a mile. Said our Lord, "If one forces you to go one mile, go with him two miles." And there has grown up in the Christian Church the expression "Going the second mile," the over-and-above, the plus accomplishments in life.

Let me retrace our steps for a few minutes and remind you anew of what the New Testament means by "love," "Thou shalt love thy neighbor," "Thou shalt love thine enemies." First, disassociate from your mind the conception of affection. It is not emotional love. There were three Greek words for love; one, *eros* — emotional love, from which we get the term *erotic*. There was the word *philos*, which means friend, from which we have the conception of friendship; and there is *agape*, Christian love. The way it was used in the new Testament and the manner it is used by us is that we are to recognize the worth of all people in the world, and their great invaluable worth in God's sight; that all men are created equal in the sight of God, that He loves all men equally as far as being His children are concerned; that we are to respect the personality of each individual in the world, even as we respect our own; that we are to have an objective approach to life, endeavoring to understand people and why they act as they do — so that if I have an enemy, in loving him, I recognize his worth in God's sight, I respect his personality no matter whether he hates me or not, I endeavor to understand why he hates me, why he acts as he does. In the language of the street, using a colloquial expression, we say we endeavor to understand what makes him "tick" in order that he acts as he does toward me and other people. Then if I love people, I am tolerant, I am patient, and if possible, I put affection into my love.

Well, there you are: recognition, respect, objectivity, tolerance, and patience—when we speak of loving a person. You see, it's perfectly possible to love a person as a Christian and not like them as individuals. However, if we work at this matter of loving people, we will in turn do what the Apostle said: Put affection into your love for the brotherhood.

Now this chapter that I read, or the portion of it, has certain points that I feel should be considered, all bearing on this whole theme of going the second mile. That is just one small point in the whole conception of our attitude toward our fellow men. It would take me a sermon for four or five Sundays to cover in part this passage; so today I can only suggest things.

First, you notice that he said, "You have heard, it hath been said of old, an eye for an eye and a tooth for a tooth; but I say unto you, resist not evil. For whosoever shall smite thee on the right cheek, turn to him the other also." Very difficult language. That old conception of an eye for an eye and a tooth for a tooth is called the *lex talionis*, the law of retaliation; and it is, I think, rather figurative, symbolic language. I do not imagine that the author of the Old Testament who wrote that meant literally that you were to knock a man's eye out or his tooth out; but they did mean that if they did you harm, you were perfectly within bounds to retaliate and do him a similar harm. The old basic problem of the feuds where one family had wronged another family, perhaps killed someone. They in turn killed a person in the first family, and they retaliated; and so before long, we had the feuds that became famous, or infamous, in our country.

That is one of the reasons why in Central Europe today these old, old countries, going back a thousand and fifteen hundred years, remember what one generation fifteen hundred years ago did to another nation or another group of people; and they still carry that hatred within their hearts. But our Lord said, Do not retaliate. If someone wrongs thee, do not retaliate.

That certainly is a religion of a mature mind. I suppose the most beautiful illustration of this to be found in literature is in those early chapters in Hugo's *Les Miserables*, where the escaped convict, Jean Valjean, spends a night in the home of the good bishop. He arises early in the morning, this convict who had escaped, and when he leaves before dawn, he takes with him all of the silverware that he could find — the bishop's silver candlesticks and other articles of worth. Before many hours he was brought back by the gendarmes, who had arrested him. When they brought him in to the presence of the bishop, they said to this man of God, Was this man your guest and did he steal this from you? The bishop replied, This man was my guest and I gave him that silver as a parting gift. The gendarmes released him; but Jean Valjean was saved in that instant. From then to the end of that marvelous book, the history of the suffering of human souls, Jean Valjean never wavered. Because a man had not retaliated he was saved by love.

I know this is hard doctrine. I am not a pacifist. I think that I do not have faith enough to be a pacifist. Thank God that there are pacifists in the world, there are men and women who are willing to take our Lord literally and hazard their lives upon this, that one should not retaliate. I say I have not yet enough faith for that; but I have watched men and women who had that faith.

I have a friend in another city who is a very distinguished judge. He is a Quaker; has been a Quaker all of his life and is the child and grandchild of Quakers. He told me one day, sitting around a table during the First World War, "Never in the history of America, from the time that William Penn came into America with his Quakers until the end of the Indian troubles, was there ever one single instance of a Quaker being killed by the Indians anywhere in the 13 colonies. They knew the Quakers were pacifists, that they would not harm the Indians; and in turn the Indians never harmed them."

I say, my friends, I have not yet enough faith to be a pacifist. But I do have faith to believe that Jesus meant this, and also that one should not retaliate; one cannot strike back in the daily affairs of life if he hopes to be a mature Christian.

Let me hurry on. He said, do not sue people at law. I am on a commission right now of our General Assembly, brought about by a very serious infraction on the part of one of our committees, wherein they sued a family, a church committee sued a family. It has caused reverberations up and down this land. It is not right for Christian people to go to law with one another. Said Jesus, never retaliate.

Then he comes to one that is very difficult. "Give to him that begs of you, and from him that would borrow of you, turn not away." You have been stopped repeatedly during the past days, perhaps, by people asking for money, for a coin or for a meal or for clothing. Today you and I are living in such a scientific age that even our charity has become scientific. We are very impersonal in our giving. We contribute to the Community Chest and to the Red Cross. You never see how that money goes. You have contributed your money; they administer it scientifically. The chances are if a person comes, we'll say, Go to this agency or that; and you pass them by. Now did Jesus mean that one is to give literally to everyone that asks him? I think this is what he means:

Certainly one is to give. Never refuse. But it doesn't say exactly what you are to give, except as Christian people, we know. You remember that one day Peter and John were going into the Temple and there was a beggar by the gate, the Gate Beautiful, who cried, "Give me alms." These two young apostles stopped and looked at him. They replied, "We have not any money. Silver and gold we have not, but we will give you something better." Then they healed him. They brought him to his feet. The beggars stopped our Lord and asked him for alms; and he healed them of palsy and of leprosy and of blindness. He healed their bodies and he healed their souls. They asked him, we'll say, for something that was perhaps worth ten dollars; in turn he gave them that which money could not buy.

So you see how it works. There may be times when it is not well to give to beggars. I personally have never been able to bring myself to that time. You may say I'm an easy mark. Never has anybody stopped me on the street that if I have money in my pockets, I do not give them something. I cannot say never; not long ago I refused, but I felt uncomfortable all the rest of the day. For after all what would a dime or a quarter be to me in giving to a poor man? But here is the point. We should seek the new perspective. No one should ever ask of us that we do not stop to find out why.

A poor man approaches us. We cannot help every poor person in the community. Here in the church we try to help many but we cannot help all. But what is the church for? Every time someone in distress asks you it probes your soul; and what do you say? Well, what causes this? Why are there people in Lexington who are poor? Why are there people living in the slums without enough to eat and enough to drink? How is it that in one community there can be people who own two and three cars and hundreds of acres of valuable property, marvelous houses, and all that they need materially — how can there within the confines of Fayette county be those who have more than they can possibly spend, and at the same time there are people in rags and destitution? Every time a poor man approaches you, you say — Why?

And I'll tell you why. Not just because some of them are useless and do-less. They are; and some of them have a heredity that they cannot overcome, and it goes back into the question of public health, and sanitation, and sterilization, and birth control — it goes back into all of those things, yes. And it goes back also into the economic order. No matter what you think of the economic order, there is something wrong that in a nation as wealthy as ours, there are poor people who need funds at any given time. Their personal weaknesses, their indolence, their heredity, their disease —

yes, all of those; but also that is part of the whole social order; and every time a man asks you for a dime, you should give to him, not necessarily the dime, though you may; but you should give to him that which Christ gave—counsel and of love and of understanding.

But more than that; it should give to you a firmer resolve that the church will take its part in making a better world. And I tell you, we shy off from those things, and we do such strange things. Today you know we are living in a very hysterical time. I marvel at the hysteria in America today. I could not possibly be a communist. You cannot be a Christian and a communist. If a man is a Christian, he cannot be a communist. I cannot be an electric light and a baptismal font at the same time. I cannot be a communist and I cannot be a Christian at the same time, because a communist says, there is no God. Well, I'm not a communist. But notice; we get hysterical, and we begin to tag people with labels; and someone differs with us just a little, is a little more liberal or inclusive economically, socially, or what-have-you; and people say, Beware, he's a Red. He's a communist. The Ku Klux rides in the South; and the Ku Klux may ride in Kentucky if we're not careful.

Or again this matter of want. Here's a man comes in and he's a "bum"; and he's been drinking. Heaven knows enough of them come to ask help from me here at the church office. Well, what caused him to be a drunkard? Some maladjustment back in his life; something; it's an effect, not a cause. You do not condemn a man because he's a drunkard; you condemn that which caused him to be a drunkard. But, here I'm trying to be a mature Christian. Do you know how much money was spent in the United States last year on education—for grade schools and high schools and colleges and universities and private schools and parochial schools—on all forms education? Why, four billion dollars. Now that's a lot of money—four billion dollars. Do you know how much money was spent on liquor in the United States in the same year—on whiskey and beer and rum and gin and all kinds of alcoholic drinks? Do you know how much money was spent? Eight billion dollars! For every dollar spent in education, two dollars on liquor. All right. Are you a mature Christian? You may be able to drink. There are thousands of people that are able to drink—I mean moderately; to no harm, apparently. But there are a lot of people who cannot. Do you know that right here in Lexington, and some of our own church members, have what? Cocktail parties. For whom? Not for people 35 and 40 and 50 years of age, but for whom? For girls and boys from 16 to 21. And I tell you, if you ever have a cocktail party and invite boys and girls from 16 to 21 and give them cocktails, you are in connivance with the devil, for you do not know whether they will be able to take it or not.

Now you're talking about giving to drunks. All right; every time you see a drunk, think back. Think back to what? Why, the cocktail parties of some of our own church members here—people whom I like and who like me, but who cannot see that they are immature. To him that asketh, turn not away; and it may be that you may have to turn to somebody that you know and say, Look here, what's wrong with your conception of society?

Now you see, this kind of talk is in the Bible—and let me hasten to add that I didn't write it. I didn't write Matthew. I didn't make these statements. Our Lord made them. I'm just telling you something about what He said. But you see, it's strong meat. Someone said to me going out of the church last Sunday, "Doctor, that's hard doctrine you're preaching today." And I replied, "You bet it's hard. You try to love your enemies, and it's a very difficult thing."

My time is practically out and I haven't talked at all about this second mile. But you see I just lead up to it. Let me suggest this: four realms of effort where we are in the second mile.

Take my life as a citizen. The first mile is what? I'm law-abiding and I pay my taxes and I vote. (I wonder how many of you voted yesterday, by the way, in your first mile?) I'm law-abiding and I pay my taxes and I vote—that's the first mile. But what's the second mile as a citizen? I inform myself of conditions in my community; I make constructive suggestions about my community; I work for constructive legislation. Never open your mouth about anything in Lexington, now, I do not care what it is — do not you open your mouth between now and next November if you didn't vote yesterday, if you failed to take the trouble to vote in the primary. Just forget any criticism because your criticism is written off. You are not even in the first mile.

Take the second mile as far as parents are concerned. As a parent what am I to do? Well, I provide material resources for my children; clothing, food, schooling and what-have-you; I give them an education — that's the first mile. But the second mile: I must know those children; I must understand children — child psychology, and how to live and work with children and go beyond just that which is apparent. I must be a friend as well as a father. I must provide in my home a spiritual atmosphere for my children, and I must also help my children to develop a disciplined life. It's just not giving them plenty of food and drink and an allowance and an education; the second mile, you see.

Consider the church. In the first mile, as a church member I am to attend the church, yes; I am to contribute, yes; I am to participate in activities, yes, and do the things that I'm asked. But the second mile as a church member is to study and to think and to work for the larger outreach of the church in the world. The church is on the march, but the church has a far larger outreach than just the worship in the sanctuary and the making the wheels go round in the organizations.

If I am going to be a second-miler with individuals, I must be just and fair with my fellow man. I must put affection into my love. It's a strange thing to remind ourselves that we can love a person as a Christian and not like them. So I must put affection into my love for the brethren if I am going the second mile.

Lately I have had many illustrations in our church of people going the second mile. Just this past week I was very much struck with someone who not only did what she should, normally, but went far beyond that which would be expected of a person in salvaging a soul and a life. Not only those things that I would be expected to do normally, but the plus, the over-and-above.

We had here in Lexington this past week Dr. Douglas Freeman — great historian, a great newspaper writer. How does Dr. Freeman do so much? He has gone the second mile with himself. He has in the attic of his house, a private sanctuary where he retires for prayer — just a little chapel of his own. He happens to be a member of the Baptist church, but he has a little private sanctuary for prayer. He's a man of very strong physical constitution. He gets up every morning at 4 o'clock; and from 4 until 8 he pursues his historical work; from 8 till 1, his newspaper work. You see he didn't get to be a great historian by just doing the ordinary routine work of his office. You do not get to be a great Christian by going just the first mile. "If a man compel thee to go with him one mile, go with him two." And after what I have said this morning, if you think that being a Christian is a simple, immature matter, you just do not have the same personality and spiritual problems that I have; for I tell you it's not a simple thing for me to be a Christian.

PROFESSED RELIGION

August 21, 1949

My meditation with you today is a logical sequence of our thoughts together during the past few Sundays. We have considered the matter of the religion of mature minds, the "strong meat" of the gospel of our Lord. Today then, the words that Jesus uttered here in the sermon called the "Sermon on the Mount" add a special emphasis to the kind of thing of which we have spoken and also help us to focus our attention on what we might call the practical side of religion. The text, then, are those words that I read to start with: "Not everyone that sayeth unto me, Lord, Lord, shall enter the Kingdom of Heaven, but he that doeth the will of my Father which is in Heaven." "Not everyone that sayeth . . . but he that doeth" is the emphasis of that statement.

Not everyone who sayeth Lord, Lord. Not all those that praise my name, said Jesus, but the ones that practice my teaching are the ones that will enter my Kingdom.

Some years ago I heard Mr. John Foster Dulles make a very interesting statement that has lingered in my mind ever since. He said it was characteristic of Americans to feel that, after they had drawn up a pact, formulated a statement, or signed an agreement, the matter was already accomplished; that if we pass a resolution, we feel that we have done that which we resolve. And as you think back into our national life during these past few decades, we see that that is all too true; all the way through our national history it has been true.We give lip service to the Declaration of Independence, then do not practice it in full by any means; we believe in the Constitution and the Bill of Rights, but all too often we honor them in the neglect of those injunctions. A few years ago we felt that we had outlawed war because such a statement was drawn up and signed by ourselves and other nations. At first we believed the League of Nations would bring world peace, then we pinned our hopes on the United Nations, and so on through life. Political parties draw up platforms, and forget them; candidates make promises, which they do not execute; church committees, General Assemblies make statements that no one ever reads; in our own church we resolve on this or that and forget it. We are prone to feel that when once we have stated an ideal, it has been accomplished, not recognizing that that is only the first step toward the realization of our dream.

Jesus, then, was very true to life when he said, "Not everyone that sayeth, Lord, Lord . . ." Not all the people who come to church and sing and pray are those that will enter my Kingdom; not at all. Now before we go further I think we should realize that problem in life in every aspect.

Educators have stated it this way: the difference between what we call "factual knowledge" and "creative living." The whole emphasis and trend of education is to translate factual knowledge into creative understanding. May I illustrate very briefly.

Here at the University we have an agricultural department, a scientific school. Men have been farming for thousands of years. It is a comparatively recent date that men have gone to school to learn how to farm, and for a long time practical farmers had very little interest in schools for farming. They said, after all, that's just a fad. Now there is a balance. A man learns by the practice of farming; he can learn more if he studies scientific farming, but he can only put into practice his knowledge of scientific farming by actu-

47

ally farming. He could stay in the University for years, take all the courses in the Ag department, never be a farmer until he actually lived on a farm or worked on a farm and practiced that which he had learned.

I read just the other day an article on the firefighters of the West.(One of the most fascinating novels that I have read in a long time is one called *Fire*, by the same man who wrote a novel called *Storm*. One was a novel of a storm, and the other of a forest fire.) Now these men are trained to fight forest fires, and those who drop from airplanes are given rigorous training, but never can they fight a fire by being parachuted down until they actually practice dropping from a plane. One does not learn how to jump out of an airplane with a parachute until he puts it into practice by doing it.

Take in the matter of surgery. (I just draw here and there for illustrations through all walks of life.) A student goes to medical college and has as his basic study that of anatomy; very exacting, difficult work it is. Those students, though, never learn to operate until they have theoretical, practical training and then they begin to operate. You do not learn to be a surgeon in your study alone.

I think back to my seminary days — how we were trained in Greek and Hebrew and Latin, English Bible, and theology and pastoral calling, all the range of studies that we had. Also there were classes in public speaking; for a minister, after all, if he is going to be a preaching minister, must have some facility in speaking, developing contact with his audience so that they will know what he is thinking and how he is trying to think with them about the Bible. At certain intervals in our seminary career we would preach a sermon before a congregation, which sermon was criticized by the faculty; and when I say criticized, I mean that they took it apart, paragraph by paragraph. If you were of a sensitive nature, it was well to stop right there, if you could not take it, as we say. No man learns to be a preacher by staying in a theological seminary all the time.

One other illustration suffices, I think. I went down the other night to a very interesting commencement exercise. It was the commencement exercises of a class in Dale Carnegie's school of speaking. I have never been to a group just like that before. I learned a lot. Now this Dale Carnegie school of speaking has a class and they meet for a number of weeks. That class runs for four hours when they meet. And why do they go? So that they may learn to speak in public, to express themselves on their feet. They are given certain rules of speech; how to organize a speech, how to prepare your materials, how to present it. Then what do they do? Why, they have to stand on the floor and speak. They learn by doing. As I listened to some of them in the competitive speeches they had, I was struck with the facility that those young men and women, some of them not quite so young, had in expressing themselves. They learned by doing.

There you are, then, you see; creative knowledge. Why did I go to school? Not to learn just an assemblage of facts. Long since I've forgotten most of the facts I learned in school. It comes to me frequently how many things I have forgotten.

One of my favorite means of relaxation is to work on the crossword puzzle of *The New York Times*, the Sunday issue of *The New York Times*. It takes encyclopedias and atlases and biographies to buttress and help you. Time and again I see some reference that I would have known 30 years ago but it has slipped my mind; particularly in Greek mythology I find that I am pretty weak, though at one time I knew the names of practically all the characters in Greek mythology. But why do I go to school? Not just to learn Greek mythology and how to read Homer in the original and how to read Virgil and Horace and Livy; how to work geometrical problems and analytical geometry and those things which I never use now. But to train my mind so that I could think and learn and acquire knowledge. Today, tomorrow and all the days — the ability to take factual knowledge and turn it into creative living; that is the aim of education.

If a student graduates from the University and has not learned to think, has not learned how to acquire fresh knowledge, how to practice that which he has learned, then you see his education failed. Our educational system has failed in many ways. For a hundred years now in Kentucky children have been required to go to school. You stop any hundred people you meet on Main Street; I daresay that half of them could not talk with you 15 minutes and use their mother tongue correctly. The solecisms and inaccuracies and mistakes in grammar that you hear on all sides! What has happened? The person has learned the factual knowledge of grammar and diction, he has not translated it into creative action; they even graduate from the University and cannot speak correctly.

Now why do I say all this? Because it is cognant to what we are talking about. Jesus said, it is not what you know about religion. That's not all that's necessary. Not your information about it, but how you use it. Now it is important to learn, and essential; necessary; but it is more important to put it into practice, for if we only know and never act, we shall not enter into the Kingdom.

May we pursue that just for a few minutes, lingering on the matter of praise, for that is what he is speaking of there. I would remind you that it is essential, absolutely requisite, to say Lord, Lord. When he says, "Not everyone that sayeth Lord, Lord . . ." he does not mean that no one should say Lord, Lord. Jesus emphasizes time and again the absolute prerequisite of saying "Lord, Lord," in other words, of praise and worship. We say that in three or four ways in church, in our homes. I would remind you of them.

We say that through hymns every Sunday, sometimes at other times. Take hymns like this: "I sing the almighty power of God," or "Lord, Thy glory fills the heavens," "Praise the Lord, ye heavens, adore Him," or "Holy, holy, holy, Lord God Almighty," "Praise god from Whom all blessing flow," and so on through the hymnal. We "Praise God." We laud and glorify His Name. We are as Isaiah in the temple of old, watching the cherubim saying, "Holy, holy, holy, Lord God almighty." One should praise God. You cannot have a religious experience in life unless you praise God. I do not mean that you cannot praise Him if you fail to sing. Some people cannot sing. They can always follow the words. Rather, they can voice within their hearts and minds the expression of the hymns.

First then, we say, "Lord, Lord" in praise. We say "Lord, Lord" also in prayer. "Our Father which art in heaven, hallowed be Thy name." Reverenced, revered, respected, loved be Thy Name. One cannot pray unless he has a sense of the magnitude, the magnificence of God. There should be awe within our souls when we approach the Mercy Seat. You remember the author of Ecclesiastes when he said, "When thou prayest, prepare thyself. Be not one that tempteth the Almighty." One cannot pray without a sense of reverence and of praise.

Then we turn to the Bible where we read such things as the Psalmist's: "Bless the Lord, O my soul, and all that is within me, bless His Holy Name"; and thus throughout the Bible. We praise God through song and prayer and Scripture and conversation. It is essential that we worship in public, yet Jesus said, while this is requisite, it is not enough. That is the point that I would drive home to myself. It is not enough to say, Lord, Lord. It is not enough to know. A further step is required.

You see then that in a way you and I are in a rather dangerous position. We are not in as dangerous a position as those who never pray and praise, for their lives have a blankness about them that is depressing and fatal; yet on the other hand we are in a slightly more dangerous place than they are, for we have learned, and if we do not perform, our house crashes about our head. Every time then you sing a hymn and voice a prayer and read the Bible and go to church, you place yourself in a slightly precarious position; that is, you may have an impulse, and not carry it out. You may be like the man whose soul was cleansed of one devil, and doing nothing, seven devils came in. If you entered church this morning with an inner need or even indifferently, and find here in the worship that which lifts you and inspires you and urges you to creative living in

51

His Kingdom, then go out of here and do nothing, it would be better that you had not come; for your soul is weaker than it was when you entered. You see, though, that that does not have to be the case. Jesus said, Do my will, the will of Him that sent me.

Well, how do we know God's will? We know it through Christ. I came, said he, not to do my own will, but the will of Him that sent me. If I want to know, then, the will of God, I study the Way of Christ; his method of living. Now I suppose the median age of our congregation is about 47; I haven't figured it out exactly, but I would say it's about 47 because we have children all the way from 10 to people past 90, and the median age would be somewhere around 47. Think how long some of us, you and I, have been saying "Lord, Lord." Piled end on end, the number of times we've been to church and the hymns we've sung and the prayers we've uttered form a staggering total. A very encouraging thing, that so many have; but now have we built on that a strong structure? I used an illustration in the pulpit ten, twelve, fifteen years ago perhaps; it came back to my mind this week. Some of you may have heard it.

A professor of theology put this in one of his books: that he had a summer home up in Michigan, and back of his summer home there was a tree that through the years grew larger and stronger and higher. Every year when he'd go back in the summer, he would compare it with the previous height. But also back there was a brush pile. Every summer they threw more brush on that pile, so that the brush pile got higher and higher and higher. The brush pile grew higher and the tree grew higher. What's the difference between a brush pile and a tree? Well, a tree, you see, is integrated, has a vitality and life and progress; and it grows. A brush pile is always only a brush pile; yet some people's lives are that way. They pile brush and brush and brush, and they get out to look at themselves and say, How I am growing. But a match just burns that brush pile, or the slightest wind blows it down.

You might come to church every Sunday for fifty years, and

52

you would build a brush pile of church attendance if there was nothing further to it. If you sing, "More love to thee, O Christ, more love to thee" — then before you go home, you needled someone; you said something unkind or you performed a deed of hatred or you cherished malice in your heart; you've sung "more love to thee" and you've performed an act of unkindness — well, what have you done? You have just put another branch on that brush pile. You've been to church one more time and your life hasn't grown. Yet you said to yourself, You know, I've been to church fifty-two times this last year; but fifty-two times this past year you may have undermined your church attendance by the things you did during the week that were malicious and hateful and unkind and unloving. That's what Jesus means, and that's what we have to watch.

So what is the touchstone of my life? As I close I would remind you of this: I am to test everything in my life by Christian love. Not by political expediency. A matter comes up and you say, Well, what's the political background of this? What party is back of it? What's the party trying to do? That's not the touchstone. You say, Is that political party acting in a Christian way? You do not test life by economic sufficiency; any measure that comes up, you do not say, Does this bring more money to me? Is there something in it for me, or is there something in it that hurts me? But — is that a Christian measure? That's the touchstone for a Christian; in politics, in economics, in society, in everything, you say to yourself, Not this external standard, but the standard of my Lord.

And sometimes you find that you cut across your political party and across your economic views and contrary to the set in which you move socially, and even to your family. That little book that came out so many years ago — *What Would Jesus Do?* — that's the touchstone of my life. So if I'm going to do that, you see, if I practice this matter, I'll find that my whole attitude will be adjusted within and without; I'll have more tolerance, I'll have more understanding, I'll have more vision, I'll have more breadth, I'll have more maturity. In other words I'll be one of those that can take the strong meat of the Gospel.

If I stop without this word, I would be discouraged myself. Always we stumble and fall; but the point is that we keep going forward, hesitantly as it may be, provided we are endeavoring to go forward. Professed Religion: Not everyone that sayeth, Lord, Lord, but he that doeth. So let us put it this way: All of us who say "Lord, Lord" — let us also do the will of Him that is our Father in heaven.

THE TWENTY-THIRD PSALM

February 5, 1950
Scripture: Psalm 23

For our morning meditation today I would speak with you on what is perhaps the most familiar passage in all of Scripture; that is, the 23rd Psalm. I have for my own information and inspiration selected four aspects of this Psalm that make it worthwhile to me and which I believe commend it to all people. I shall not consider the latter part of the Psalm, only that portion where the writer compares our Lord to a Shepherd.

Why is it that people all over the world repeat the 23rd Psalm, learn it by heart, want it in time of joy, desire it in periods of suffering and mourning, use it for inspiration and for a stay throughout the days? To me it has been of priceless value. I would share with you then the four aspects of the Psalm that have made it so worthwhile for me in my own living.

Four words illustrate what I mean: rest, refreshing, righteousness, and resolution. Rest, refreshing, righteousness, and resolution. May we look at them very briefly. "The Lord is my shepherd; I shall not want. He maketh me to lie down in green pastures." Palestine was an arid country; it still is an arid country for

55

the most part, though marvelous things have been done there in recent years to make it blossom as a rose. Along these dry wastes a shepherd sought out the riverbrooks where there would be green pastures for his sheep. He was speaking here of a place to rest, for physical rest and for spiritual rest, if you will.

Some years ago now I saw for the first time that very remarkable play, *Green Pastures.* We recognize that one of the best mediums in art for promulgating the teaching and presenting stimulating aspects of life is found on the stage. On a hot August day I attended the play in New York City. *Green Pastures* had such an appeal for people because it was the illustration of the search on the part of a race for rest, for physical rest, spiritual refreshment. The author caught the desire for those people; he pictured for us and for them the scene of green pastures where a man can lie down and find rest unto his soul. "He maketh me to lie down in green pastures."

Later on our Lord said, "I am the good shepherd." Then one day He uttered what is perhaps the greatest of all His sayings: "Come unto me, all ye that labor and are heavy-laden, and I will give you rest. Take my yoke upon you and learn of me, for I am meek and lowly in spirit, and ye shall find rest unto your souls." Jesus Christ promised us that we will find rest unto our souls, provided we take His yoke upon us. And as we have seen so often, a yoke is that which disciplines, provides companionship, and affords direction; for two oxen under the yoke have the discipline of the yoke, the fellowship of kindred effort, and the purpose that lies before them.

In our Christian living, my friends, we find rest when we accept the discipline of the Lord Christ; when we are yoked with Him in the common purpose of His Kingdom; when we march on from day to day toward the objective of His teachings. The Lord makes us to lie down in green pastures; he provides rest unto our souls.

As we leave that, might I remind you of the common saying that "Other pastures always look greener." There is a restlessness in our lives that causes us to look over the fences of our own pasture into others. We say that if we could change our situation or our environment or our circumstances, life would be fairer and brighter and greener. We are hemmed in by circumstances; we are defeated by fate. Just another chance, it would be better. That's not the way life is. We live where we are. Where we find ourselves today, we live our lives; and we will attain this rest and these green pastures provided we give ourselves to the yoke of the Lord Christ.

There is a startling statement in the Book of Revelation that shows the opposite of that. The writer is describing people who have no rest: "And they have no rest night nor day, who have the mark of the beast upon them" or "who worship the beast," either way you want it. They have no rest neither day nor night, those that have the mark of the beast upon them. In other words, the writer of that symbolical book reminds us that if evil in our lives is in the ascendant, if we have given ourselves over, even negatively, to that which is wrong, there is no rest. We are defeated, we are restless, because of the evil on the throne of our lives.

When Coleridge wrote his "Ancient Mariner," he developed that. The Ancient Mariner could find no peace in his soul because of the remorse that he had for his sin. And also when we read Eugene Sue's "The Wandering Jew," the man who wandered all over the world year after year after year, century after century, because when our Lord was on the way to Golgotha, he had spat upon Him and derided Him. No rest for those that have a sense of guilt, but Jesus, you see, says this: All men are guilty. Paul reminded us: All have sinned and fallen short, but Jesus Christ is able and willing and ready to forgive us our sins. Every man sins, but those that recognize it and in due humility repent and confess their sins to God, find peace. "My yoke . . . ye shall find peace and rest unto your souls.

The Psalmist says, "He maketh me to lie down in green pastures." The first word to remember about the 23rd Psalm is "rest." The second word is "refreshing."

Refreshing. "He restoreth my soul." He restoreth my soul, having led me beside the still waters. Again it is a very difficult thing to live in a land where there is no water. Our friends in New York have been experiencing it. Just last night at the manse the hot water boiler broke in the middle of the night and we had to turn it off; we have no water at home today. That is quite an annoyance to live with no water. "He leadeth me beside the still waters," where I can find refreshment. Everyone in that country understood what it meant to have quiet deep waters.

Years ago someone gave me a very lovely print of the 23rd Psalm; it hangs in my study on the wall. The shepherd leading his flock through a vale, water flowing along; a quiet, restful scene. I let my eyes fall upon it from time to time just to imbibe the restfulness and the restoration conveyed by that picture. Now if I am going to find refreshing, I go with him. And the author employs in the New Testament when he says that "I am the good shepherd" a word that means "feeder." "I am the good feeder," said our Lord. "I feed my sheep." He feeds you and me.

Back in the seventeenth century when John Milton was commemorating the death of his dear friend in that remarkable poem, "Lycidas," he goes on to talk about church leaders who were unworthy. He says this about the church leaders of that day: "The hungry sheep look up, and are not fed." No sheep, though, ever looked toward our Lord without finding the food and the drink necessary for the soul. He feeds me in various ways.

Recently I had two little girls in my study on Sunday morning with their mother to talk about what it means to be a Christian. They were going away, and could not be in the communicant's class later. The other day I took them in front of the fireplace to look at daVinci's picture of our Lord and His twelve friends at the first communion table. You remember it so well, painted on the refectory wall of a monastery in the city of Milan. Always through the years, the Lord's Supper has been a symbol that Christ feeds our spiritual bodies, even as bread and meat feed our physical bodies. I will find refreshing through that symbolism, and through a belief in God, and through the possibilities of good in man that Jesus has demonstrated, and in the possibilities of good in myself.

Last week you know I talked with you about being bored. I would remind you also that people become discouraged at times. We are as Elijah, thinking that perhaps we are the only ones left in the world that worship God, and then always God shows us there are seven thousand that have not bowed to Baal. We find refreshing through this ever-recurrence of the possibilities of good in every human being. No one ever thinks of himself as being purely evil. Everybody, nearly, wants to do that which is right. Through a combination of circumstances we fail to, quite often, but there are untold possibilities for good in human beings, and Jesus Christ points them up all the time. No matter who it is, if you place him against the background of our Lord, you will find this: that imperfections will be shown, but also through the radiation of the love of Christ, positive virtues will come out of which you never dreamed. He feeds our souls by reminding us of the good in everyone, then of the good in myself.

The second thing then in the 23rd Psalm is "refreshing." "He leadeth me beside the still waters; he restoreth my soul." The third is, "He leadeth me in the paths of righteousness for his name's sake." Righteousness, the right way. A sheep is apt to be lost. Silly sheep, we say, and they go in all directions following a leader. The way is very difficult for a sheep to find. Now a shepherd leads them in the right way, "righteousness" meaning the right way. They get lost; everyone gets lost. I suppose this story is an apocryphal one, but it is reported that someone asked Daniel Boone once if he had ever gotten lost in the wilderness of Kentucky when he was wandering around in this state in the early days. Boone considered for a moment and said, No, he had never been lost, but once he had been confused for about three days. That, you see, is the way we are; all of us get confused. We may not lose the way completely, but we are confused and we must circle around to find it.

59

How very confused we get, you and I.

After all, what is right, and what is wrong? When is an action right, and when is it evil? How can I follow the right way in life? Of course we have certain norms, such as the Ten Commandments, but they have to be understood pretty carefully. We have other general precepts, but they have to be understood. Our Lord gave us the key, I think, to right living. When you study His words, you find this: he seldom applies a teaching to a particular situation, or rather he does not give particular laws for particular situations. He had general truths, such as loving thy neighbor, and being kind one to another, and not resenting wrong, and conquering anger, and turning the other cheek; not hating anyone, either enemy or friend. Then you see, those general laws are put at the particular point that we need them. When he told the story of the Good Samaritan to illustrate the love of neighbors, then as I go into Lexington this week, I must apply that story to particular situations as they arise. You see it takes a little thought and a little understanding and constant application.

If you follow the teaching of our Lord, you will discover this, I believe: that in His eye, right living consists primarily of proper attitudes and contacts with one's fellows. In other words, righteousness is right living toward one's fellow man. Thou shalt love the Lord thy God even as thou dost love thyself, and express it through thy love to thy neighbor. Righteousness, right living, with our fellow men.

May I use a very simple illustration. The other day I was calling at St. Joseph's hospital on two or three of our members who were sick. It was late in the afternoon and I was crowded for time. When I crossed Jefferson Street going west I noticed that all the way from Jefferson Street to Georgetown, cars were parked solidly on the left hand side. Second Street, you remember, is a one-way street going west. On the right hand side it was empty; I take it back—about one car. So I wanted to see these people, I had a limited amount of time, drew up on the right hand side and hopped out and went into the hospital where I stayed about ten minutes. When I came back, there was a tag on my car from the police for parking on the wrong side of the street. Signs all along: "No parking on this side."

So I put the card in my pocket, forgot it, and they sent me a reminder. I phoned them and said, Now I'm going to come by and pay this dollar, but I wish you would give me an explanation of why it is that on a street that is a one-way street and people are using it all the time, that you will allow cars to park only on the left and not on the right? I'm just curious when I pay this dollar that I owe you. The girl gave me an answer, and a very good answer. Said she, They keep the right hand side of Second Street free of cars; for if a fire broke out in St. Joseph's hospital, they would need that side of the street to be empty for the fire equipment — an excellent reason.

Now I had sinned against the traffic laws of Lexington, for which I make restitution — a dollar — and also learn a lesson, I hope. But it was a very sound reason. I broke a traffic law, but the traffic law was fixed so that my fellow citizens could be protected; and it might have been that my car there that afternoon would have caused a loss of life on the part of somebody in St. Joe's if a fire had broken out. I do not have to labor the illustration.

That is what wrongdoing is in life. I break the laws of living when I injure my fellow man; and when I injure him, it reacts on myself. So He leads me in the paths of right living; I do not move away when I follow our Lord. And all of life has traffic laws to guide us along the highways of the days, and Our Lord is the shepherd that leads us. So you see we find rest, and restoration, and righteousness.

The last thing that we find, or that I would mention, is resolution. Dr. Moffat translates those words very well. Let me read to you those of the King James: "Yea, though I walk through the valley of the shadow of death, I will fear no evil, for thou art with me. Thy rod and thy staff they comfort me." That does not mean through the valley of death, but through the valley of the shadow of death, which is a different thing—through the valley of fear. "Yea, though I walk through the valley of fear, thou dost comfort me." Dr. Moffat has it, "My road may run through a glen of gloom, but I fear no harm, for thou art beside me, thy club, thy staff, they give me courage." "They give me courage." So this Psalm gives men courage. "Though I walk through a glen of gloom . . ." we have resolution. Now for me that is the key to the whole poem.

Everyone is afraid, at times. Courage of course would be the mean between foolhardiness and timidity. A foolhardy man on one side and timid man on the other would not be valuable, but a courageous man in between. But all of us are fearful. We may be fearful of health, or of financial security, or of many things, and this Psalm helps us on the way. "Though I walk through the valley of fear, thou art with me." And how does He give us courage? I would remind you of this: the example of how He met life. The trouble in our thinking of our Lord is that we have put so many theological interpretations on His life that we forget the fact that He was a young man, that He wanted to live, that He enjoyed health and that He was filled with a great zest, and He had to die when He was barely thirty. We forget the courage that it took to face it. He faced the problem of being unpopular, and He faced the problem of physical fatigue, and being misunderstood, and being betrayed—nothing that can happen to us in a negative way did not happen to Him. So if I follow this shepherd, I have the inspiration from Him to bolster my courage.

Then I have the strength that comes from these eternal purposes. It is a good thing to believe that there is purpose in the universe, that there is a divinity that shapes our ends, that there is a general ongoing of life, and that all things do work together for good to those that love God. I say it is a heartening belief. So I know that whate'er betide, life moves toward the proper consummation. Sometimes we become very anxious and concerned. Let us rest in God.

Just last year I was in a conference in the East and saw an old friend of mine who had moved East and was preaching there. We had lunch together, this seminary mate, just three years younger than I am. I remember a sermon that he preached in which he was talking about a businessman who had told him that he tried to live so that no matter what eventuality came, whether he had bad news about his business or his family, whatever it was, that he had built up inner resources to meet that. That sermon has lingered in my mind over the years. Two weeks ago I heard that this friend of mine had died—a man in his middle fifties stricken down by a fatal illness. As I thought of it, I realized that he himself was ready, that it was not merely speaking on his part, but he had that inner strength to meet any eventuality, including death. "I will fear not, if thou art with me."

The companionship of other people helps at that point. I quote *Pilgrim's Progress* so often that I sometimes feel that you must think I do nothing but read *Pilgrim's Progress;* but I would hate to give it up. It is one of my ten best books. When Christian left the Interpreter's house, going toward the Delectable Mountains that he had seen from the roof in the morning, he went down at once into the Valley of the Shadow of Death, into the darkness and dread of that dreary glen. As he walked in the fog and the darkness, he was frightened. But Bunyan brings two helps to bear. Christian heard around him in the darkness the voices of others calling to him, and calling to one another, encouraging each other. I think sometimes that the very best Christian service anyone can render is to be mindful to drop a word of encouragement through the days. You never know when just some chance word will help. When someone passes on a pleasantry or a cheerful word to me, I have a lift of spirit at once. So in this weary glen, we prize the companionship of others.

Then when he met Appolyon, you remember. He hit Appolyon with everything in the book, but Appolyon still kept on. Then, said Bunyan, Christian drew that final weapon, All-Prayer, and with All-Prayer, he conquered the Devil. In this valley of fear, prayer, All-Prayer.

The next time you are frightened, the next time you cannot sleep, when you wake in those small hours of the night and feel pressed and fearful, just repeat these words; and when you come to "Yea, though I walk through the valley of the shadow of death, I will fear no evil," remind yourself in modern parlance, "If the shepherd is with me, so what?"

There is the Psalm as I see it—four words. "The Lord is my shepherd. He gives me rest, and refreshing, righteousness, and resolution." May we make these four R's our guiding points throughout the week.

SEARCH
AFTER
TRUTH

February 26, 1950
Scripture: Amos 5:21-27

Continuing our meditations in the description of Christianity by our Lord, I would have you use as the background of your thinking this morning the words in the Beatitudes that read as follows: "Blessed are they that hunger and thirst after righteousness, for they shall be filled."

We have seen so far in our discussion of the interpretation of Christianity by our Lord, the first step was to repent; that man must have a change of mind, a willingness to realize his mistakes, above all to admit them, and in humility of heart, seek forgiveness and renewal. Then last week we came to the last step; that of a recognition and realization on our part of our spiritual inadequacy ("Blessed are the poor in spirit, for theirs is the Kingdom of God").

Today we go a step further, as it were; perhaps a more positive emphasis than before, when He said, "Blessed are they that hunger and thirst after righteousness, for they shall be filled." Following our usual custom, let us examine these words for a moment. "Blessed" of course meaning "happy" is the man; and one who hungers and thirsts craves ardently for a matter. Perhaps we

65

might say, those that have a passion for righteousness, that desire it above all other things in life. As far as the word employed in the New Testament for "righteousness," it has a three-pronged meaning. The Greek word here has this emphasis: correctness in thinking, feeling, and acting. Righteousness, according to the Greek, would be correctness; correctness in our thinking, in our feeling, in our acting; an intellectual, emotional, and volitional approach.

The verse then means something like this: Happy are those that have a passion for correctness in thinking, feeling, and acting; for they shall be recompensed or filled. You notice that we had for our First Lesson today words from the prophet Amos. That prophet of long ago writing some seven hundred years before our Lord is the one that is known primarily for the note that he sounded on righteousness. There arose in that eighth century before Christ a remarkable coterie of men, the Hebrew prophets who have never been excelled in spiritual insight; nor has anyone ever bettered their expression of great spiritual values. Amos, known for his emphasis on righteousness; Micah, on justice, mercy; Hosea on love; righteousness, justice, mercy, humility, love. These men have spoken so that all through the ages their fellows have listened. Mature conceptions thrown into the world long before the days of our Lord.

Then when Jesus came, he took these statements and these conceptions of righteousness, mercy, justice, humility, and love; I say, he took them and clothed them with his own experience, demonstrating to the world that they could be lived, and left for us a definite example of the possibilities of that kind of life.

When Amos spoke of righteousness, he gave to his fellow countrymen a conception that they had never had before, of the absolute rightness of God. They had felt that God was a national one, that Jehovah was a God of the Jews, but not of other people; that He was a whimsical God, if you will, a deity that could be persuaded to favor His own people. Amos brought to their attention the fact that God was absolutely righteous, that there was righteousness inherent in the Deity, that as far as He Himself was concerned there was no turning away from that which is right; nor could He accept anything less than righteousness on the part of His people. They could not placate Him by formalism and sacrifices. "I despise your burnt offerings," Amos made Him say. Not by form nor ceremony nor sacrifice is God to be worshipped, but with humility and love. And there in that passage that we read Amos told them, for God, that they must let righteousness flow down their streets as water, that it must be as common as water, it must be as ongoing and healing and constructive as water itself.

Then Amos brought a very interesting figure of speech into the discussion. He said, God is holding a plumbline on Israel, even as a man holds a plumbline to find whether a wall is true or not; so God holds a plumbline in His people — to see if they measure the righteousness of God. God, then, is One Who is right; He is universal and not particular. He is law-abiding, not whimsical; He is worshipped, not primarily through form, but through the inwardness of a man's attitude.

Might we keep that in the back of our minds as we notice how our Lord built upon that and went on from it into His great pronouncement concerning righteous living. Happy, said He, is the man that hungers and thirsts after righteousness; who craves ardently after it; who has a passion for righteousness.

There are two great hungers in the human race, these hungers that enable the race to live and to propagate itself. If there were not two basic, inherent hungers in the human race, it would not continue. One of those hungers is for food and drink, and the other is the hunger that we call sex hunger. One to preserve life, one to perpetuate the generation. These are basic, driving urges in every human being. We know that if these hungers are not disciplined, they lead to disaster; that there must be temperance in both, in the expression and the feeding of both, yet we recognize that they are there. Jesus used one for his illustration. Even as a man hungers, and eats and drinks that he may live, even as he desires food for life, so he must desire righteousness if he is going to have

67

spiritual life. There must be a passion in a man for righteousness. I trust we will remember that; that we will have that ardent hunger for that which is true and righteous altogether.

You and I live in an age that is called the Scientific Age. In this Scientific Age men have had a great desire for truth. They have sought after truth passionately. They have "scorned delight, and lived laborious days" in order that they might discover truth. I was reading just the other day the review of a new life of Pasteur. Mothers and fathers in our midst, whose small children follow the way of growth, who are beset by many germs and physical ailments, have more to thank Pasteur for than almost any man in the field of science. When we think of the pasteurization of drink, and the cure of rabies — those two are enough — we see what debtors the human race, what debtors we are to Pasteur. He was a man not only of great mind but a great heart. He gave himself with passionate endeavor to the discovery of truth. Happy is the man who has a passion for discovery of truth; they will scorn delight, and live laborious days, that the end may be achieved.

We know though that there are not only laws that are physical but that there are moral laws as well. This world is built on physical laws; it is also composed of the moral laws, that which we can see and touch; that which we can feel and understand. Might I remind you briefly of where we look for moral law. We discover scientific laws in textbooks and laboratories and test tubes and formulas; we follow along the trail that has been blazed by others and we take step by step in the new truth, or rather in the discovery of truth; for truth has been there always. In the moral law we have a textbook and illustrations. We have the Ten Words of Moses, that give these tested formulas of how one should live in society, his attitude toward God, his attitude toward his family, his relation with other people, respecting their property and their life and their good name; our relationship to God and neighbor, transmuted as it were through our contacts with our family.

Then we saw how these Hebrew prophets went beyond that

and spoke of righteousness and justice and humility and mercy and love. Then Jesus went beyond that, and told us what love is in life; how one loves his fellowman by recognizing his worth, respecting him as a personality, and expressing his righteousness, not in a vacuum; demonstrating his righteousness within and toward God through his relationship with his fellow man. One does not live alone, apart or separate from life; for righteousness is in our relationship with our fellow man.

Now, said our Lord, we must give ourselves passionately, ardently, to the search after righteousness. We must hunger after it. If Pasteur and Einstein, all the glorious company of scientists, can give themselves ardently to the discovery of truth, so we, who may or may not be scientists, who may or may not be learned, who may have had opportunities or not, you and I, the human race, is to give itself; we are to give ourselves, ardently, passionately — the great hunger and thirst after the discovery of the application of righteousness in living. Only as people do that can the kingdom of heaven be built, and spread; only then can it grow in my own life and in the life of those around me.

Happy is the man that has a passion for righteousness. This word then that we use, this term "righteousness," as we saw, means correctness; that which is correct, rather than that which is wrong. That which is right, over against that which is in error. Right in the moral sense of living. Let me seek that which is right over against that which is wrong, and let me do it with such a passion of soul that I will subordinate everything to that kind of living. Correctness in three ways: in my thinking, in my feeling, in my acting.

Let me have a love for truth. May I have a respect for truth. may I give myself not only to the search and the love and respect, but may I follow after truth. A young person in a university, if he does not have a passion for knowledge and for truth, might just as well be somewhere else. Think of the time and money wasted by those who have no desire for truth. Not only in universities, but everywhere, we should have a desire for the truth. The church of the living God should be the great exponent of truth. Our Lord said, I am Truth. He was Truth; He is Truth. Those who follow after Him should think in terms of truth.

I was reminded the other day of one of the great mistakes the Church has made through the medium of a crossword puzzle. I like to relax at times in working crossword puzzles; the one in the Sunday edition of *The New York Times* stretches my intelligence. It may be child's play for you. And one of the questions was: How were Galileo's discoveries thought of? And the answer of course was that they were heresies. The Church, when Galileo made his pronouncements of physical discoveries and his investigations or experiments about the pendulum and gravity and acceleration and so on; why, said the doctors of the Church, these things cannot be. They are not true. And Galileo, who knew that they were true because he had proved them, was forced to recant. The Church had set itself against truth. The Church fought the theories of Copernicus; the Church fought the theories of Darwin; the Church throughout the centuries all too often has set itself against truth because it has preconceived notions. My brethren, if we have a hunger after righteousness, let us see to it that we have a hunger after truth; and do not pre-judge any situation in the field of morals. Pre-judge nothing, and when we pre-judge, we are guilty of prejudice.

A righteous man, then, desires the truth, no matter where it leads. Remember this, though: that Almighty God is true and righteous altogether. Truth will never lead a man away from his God, although it may cut across his preconceived ideas.

The second part of righteousness is not only correctness in thinking but correctness in feeling; have an emotional reaction to truth. That seems in a way rather a strange emphasis on truth, yet one should have an emotional reaction that is proper for truth. How do I feel? What is my emotional content? Do I understand mercy and love and righteousness and justice? Do I have not only an intellectual appreciation but an emotional response? Do I love with my heart as well as conceive with my mind?

I suppose that many of you did what I did this past week and the week before—went out to the University to take part in the dedication of that beautiful building we have of which we are proud and which has such possibilities for constructive service. And there we saw the old Greek play, *Medea*. What an experience to sit through that performance. In the intermission I was in the lobby drinking coffee with some friends in the ministry and one of the deans at the University said to us present, Well gentlemen, what material are you getting from this for your sermon? I looked at my ministerial friend, smiled and replied, Well, the way I would express it is this: Medea showed absolutely a life without love, without the virtue of love; of revenge, justice without love. The other man smiled and said, I think you've hit the nail on the head. Medea was wronged. Her husband betrayed her; he left her for another woman, forsook his children, and she hated him for it. Not only did she hate him for it, but she said, I will destroy him; I'll have my revenge. An eye for an eye and a tooth for a tooth. If thine enemy hit thee, return the blow. If he knock out an eye, knock out his eye. To get even with a man; "I'll get even with you," says someone. "I'll pay you back." Medea set out, so that she killed the woman he was to marry, and her father, and then to destroy him, she killed her own children—the hatred, the revenge that welled up in that poor woman's life. Hatred, revenge; but righteousness says, Thou shalt love thy neighbor. It goes beyond that. Thou shalt love them that despitefully use you. What a strange injunction. So righteousness involves feeling, an emotional response. I must weep over the lost sheep of Israel; I must weep over my enemies; above all, I must weep over my own shortcomings. God grant that our hearts may be stirred emotionally as we consider the matter of righteousness.

Ah, but it is not only an act of thinking or of feeling. It is correctness in action. And that brings us you see where all of these meditations convey us, to the word "do." I must not only be; I must *do*. First I must be; but then I must do. There is no completion without activity. I can recognize that which is right; I can have the great emotional surge for that which is right; but I shall as Hamlet lose myself in a labyrinth of thought and indecision unless I bring myself to the sticking point of action; of action in His kingdom. This *do*, and thou shalt live. He that *doeth* the will of my Father . . . He that heareth these words and *doeth* them.

Do I have a passion for righteousness? Correctness in my attitude toward all my fellow men in Lexington, all my fellowmen in the world, toward everyone, toward myself? Then, God willing, I must apply it. I need brains, yes; all the brains that I have. I need feeling, yes; all of the emotional content that I can. But I must do; I must do.

Might I use this illustration as we close. They asked us today to mention the fact of the problem of drinking. Certainly I am not preaching a sermon on that but it is an illustration we can use. Do I have a hunger and thirst after righteousness in living, in correctness? Do I think clearly into the matter of all the problems of alcoholism, from the mere social drink to the confirmed alcoholic? Do I have an emotional content about those that it harms and what it does to them, what it may do to me? Do I act on it?

If you ever think, for instance, of having a cocktail party for a high school group of boys and girls, boys and girls from 15 to 20, do you have intelligence to understand what that may do to just one of those boys or girls? Have you an emotional experience to suffer with some alcoholic, and have tried through the grace of God to help him? Are you willing to say regardless of what society does, I shall not be a party to tempting some young person? You see, you may phrase as many pious platitudes as you want to. You may weep over the problems of your family and you friends, but I tell you in God's name, if you are not willing to *do* something about it, you never approach the real point.

Happy is the man, said our Lord, who has a passion, who has a passion for correctness in thinking, in feeling, and in action. Blessed are those that hunger and thirst after righteousness, for the reward is that they will be filled; they will find their heart's desire.

GALLANT AND HIGH HEARTED HAPPINESS

March 5, 1950
Scripture: Psalm 67

Continuing our meditations on the characteristics of a Christian or the cardinal precepts of Christianity, as outlined by our Lord, we come today to that Beatitude, "Blessed are the merciful, for they shall obtain mercy."

Blessed are the merciful, for they shall obtain mercy. It is very difficult to differentiate between the characteristics of a Christian, to say which is the most important, which should be elevated above all others. Perhaps as we have followed this, we have discovered that one characteristic is essential above all others. That is, the one that we call "humility." We have seen that Christ started His Beatitudes with the saying, "Blessed are the poor in spirit, for theirs is the kingdom of heaven." One who is poor in spirit recognizes his spiritual inadequacy; he has humility. Until one has humility, he is not willing to admit his mistakes; and until one acknowledges his mistakes, he will not repent nor can he be forgiven. Humility then is the keystone to the entire approach of Christianity. Unless a man is humble, he cannot see the Kingdom of God.

I daresay the one today runs it a close second, reminding

73

you that we cannot differentiate between these too closely. "Blessed are the merciful." And the word *mercy* means, in our language, forbearance, or a disinclination to inflict harm under any circumstances. When we speak of "merciful," we mean compassionate, tender, humane, gracious, kind. Blessed are the compassionate; happy are those that are kind. I daresay then that kindness runs a close second to humility. If one is humble, he is predisposed to be kind. Without kindness in the world, very little can be done in building a Christian way. Rather, if one is not kind, he could hardly be described as a Christian.

It is an interesting thing how that word has crept into our language. Going back to the Greek work "elios," meaning mercy, we have taken it bodily and placed it in our language. We talk about "eleemosynary" institutions. An eleemosynary institution is one where charity is demonstrated. Insane asylums, hospitals for the poor, hospitals for the unfortunate, all kinds of institutions and services for people in need are called eleemosynary institutions. We have Red Cross drives, Community Chest drives, and crippled children's hospitals and polio drives. Every time you turn around, nearly, you are confronted with some organization that is an eleemosynary one—interested in the unfortunate, endeavoring to help those that need. That is a day by day demonstration of what our Lord meant when He said, Happy are those that are merciful. If it were not for Christian mercy, we would not have that kind of an undertaking.

I say then this is a household understanding. It does not need much elaboration. When you are kind, you are disposed to do good, and confer happiness. A man that is kind wishes to confer happiness. Anyone that is kind is predisposed to do good. Happy is the man, then that wishes to confer happiness on people; for that is part of our Christian life.

I would remind you that in the Christian conception we believe that the mercy of God is one of His attributes. You can pick up the Scriptures almost anywhere and discover that. It seems to me the Psalmists, those men who wrote the hymns of Israel, voiced it better than anyone else. "Surely Goodness and mercy shall follow me all the days of my life." "All the paths of the Lord are mercy." "The mercy of the Lord is from everlasting to everlasting." "He is good, for His mercy endureth forever." And then Paul said "that He might have mercy upon all." You see, when men think of God, they picture that which is merciful: charity, love, the outreach of His love to touch us in our need.

Back in Hosea he makes God say this: "I shall be as the dew upon Israel." I do not know whether Shakespeare was thinking of that when he wrote those lines,

> The quality of mercy is not strained.
> It droppeth as the gentle rain
> From heaven upon the place beneath.
> It is twice blessed. It blesseth him that gives
> And him that takes. 'Tis mightiest in the mighty.

"It droppeth as the gentle rain from heaven," and Hosea said, "I shall be as the dew upon Israel." Sometimes when I try to decide what line in poetry I love above all others, I find one that fits a mood, and then there will be another one that will touch me. I daresay that all of us are that way, for that is the appeal of poetry; many moods, many expressions. However, it seems to me that if there were one line in English poetry that I would rather have upon my tomb for an epitaph than any other, it is the one that Matthew Arnold wrote about his father, about Rugby Chapel:

> Thou wouldst not *alone* be saved, my father;
> Alone, conquer and come to the grave.

Then he goes on to tell how the father had turned and given a helping hand to the unfortunate souls that stumbled upon the way. "Thou wouldst not alone be saved." The mercy of God is transmuted through the mercy of individuals, the love of God in action, the kindness of God, if you will.

Pearl Buck has said somewhere that she considered kindness as the outstanding Christian virtue. She grew up in China; she knew the sorrow and suffering of that nation, and she knew from observation the need for kindness. The love of the Eternal is most wonderfully kind, we sing. It is well to drive back into our thoughts all the time that God is merciful, that God loves us, God is there.

Now one cannot picture God very well. As far as these personal attributes are concerned, He is a personality. He has no body; He is not a man. We think of Him as Intelligence and Spirit. The only way I can come to a concrete understanding of God is through Christ. You see there is always in the back on one's mind an "if" about God. That may sound strange. You cannot demonstrate God. You believe in Him. You believe there is order and purpose in this universe but you cannot prove it. You simply cannot prove the existence of God beyond any philosophical or scientific shadow of a doubt. I believe absolutely in the Personality and the Presence of God. As Donald Hankey said years ago, "Faith is betting one's life that there is a God." One builds his whole philosophy on the fact of God.

But I do know the fact of Christ. We read today in the First Lesson how Christ said that "He that hath seen me hath seen the Father." He identified himself with God — spiritually, I mean. So Christ is all the God-conception one needs; that is, conception for life. Whatever made Christ possible is God. The kind of life that Christ lived had its inception somewhere, and that inception we call God. So one need not be too concerned about the philosophical hair-splitting and theological problems. Take hold on Christ, on the fact of Christ. He leads me to God.

Now Christ had compassion. He was merciful. We find over and over again how he was moved with compassion for the lost sheep of Israel; he wept over Jerusalem; he wept over Capernaum.

He spent hours healing men's bodies, ministering to their spirits, helping their souls. He was moved with compassion, with love. So God is merciful, for Christ was merciful. Or if you want to reverse it, Christ was merciful, for God is merciful. A Christian endeavors to reflect and emulate the compassion of his Lord.

Now you know Christianity is a very difficult thing. If you do not know how difficult it is, just try to preach and try to decide whether you think these statements are facts. And when I prepare sermons, I have to give more thought to it than you who listen and have to sift very carefully whether I am speaking truth or hearsay. Someone stopped me last Sunday after church and said, "Now you talk about this matter of love, of loving your fellow man. Dr. Miles, am I supposed to love Joe Stalin?" There you are. Are you supposed to love Joe Stalin? And how can you love him? When you put yourself down in front of a concrete problem, do you suppose God feels merciful toward those men?

Years ago I read a story I have quoted here; it's worth quoting again, of a famous scholar in France during the Reformation who fled from France. He landed in the city of Milan, where he was taken sick and nearly died. They placed him in a hospital. He was in rags, lying on the floor. And two doctors came in. They looked at this man who was nearly unconscious, clothed in rags and covered with dirt. Said one doctor to the other, "This miserable wretch is going to die." And Murutus to their amazement replied in very choice Latin, "Call no man miserable for whom Christ did not disdain to die."

So you see when you are confronted with the problem of whether you can love Joe Stalin, the first thing you have to remember is this: that on Golgotha, Jesus Christ died for Joe Stalin, just as much as he died for R.W. Miles. Now that's rather an humbling feeling. I haven't murdered a lot of people as we think he has; I haven't tried to inflict my way on millions of people. But Christ died for him as much as He did for me. My brethren, if we are Christian, we are going to be compassionate. It does not say that I am to love what Joe Stalin does, the effect of his life; but it does say that I am to recognize the fact that the mercy of God has been exemplified and demonstrated for him as much as for me. And somewhere — do not worry — but somewhere, before all the results are in, we do not know when or how, but we can believe Paul when he said, "that He might have mercy upon all."Not upon some; not upon Americans; not upon white people; not upon Presbyterians — Paul very definitely says that God will have mercy upon *all*. "All" means *all*. So God will save Joe Stalin in His good time, do not worry. He would not be saved if it were left to us, you see; but the mercy of God never let anybody go. Not anybody, anywhere, any time. It is inclusive for all. You say, where is the Scripture for it? There is the Scripture for it. Paul said it right there. God's mercy would reach all men eventually.

Well then, if God is merciful, if God is compassionate, if He is loving and kind, what am I to do, man to man? Are we to express kindness and mercy and love. One of the writers in this country, William Allen White, a very famous newspaper man, great friend of Governor Allen of Kansas, one of the greatest Republican writers, perhaps, in this century, talked about the "wisdom of kindness." The wisdom of kindness, in all relations — labor, capital, social, economic, anywhere; that to be kind is to be wise, for people work together so much better through kindness.

Am I then disposed to do good? For if I am, I am kind. There is a prayer that hangs on my study wall that has this sentence: "Strengthen the good thing thus begun, that with gallant and high-hearted happiness we may work for Thy kingdom in the hearts of men." "With gallant and high-hearted happiness" we may work for the kingdom of God in the hearts of men. High-hearted happiness comes from kindness.

I was riding out to the airport the other day and noticed the Crippled Children's convalescent hospital that is nearly completed. Why was it put there? How was it put there? Because people are kind. They love their fellow men. I called on a little girl not long ago in the Shriners' Hospital, children in traction and casts and so on; happy. Why were they there? How were they there? Because men are kind. You go to this kind of a Home or that, and you find that people are helped. And why? Because men are kind. They are merciful.

Now Jesus said, Happy is the man that is compassionate, that is kind, who is disposed to do good, who wants to help. What is your reaction when someone asks you for assistance? It's always a pretty good test. Sometimes you cannot help them. You know that perhaps you should not help them. But are you sympathetic? Are you friendly? Do you want to help, do you want to do some good?

Yesterday I said to a man who was in my study, I want you to run an errand for me. Here is someone in need. And I told him about a man that he had never heard of, but the man was in jail. He was in jail for robbery, and armed; a very serious offense. "Can you call on that man this afternoon?" said I. Well, before dinner he phoned me that he had called at the jail on that man. He was kind and compassionate. You never know, you never know when you are going to need somebody to be kind to you. We walk along very proudly, but there's no one that may not sometimes fall. There may be a time when you feel that all men's hands are against you, but if someone is kind, you'll never forget it. And not only will you not forget it; neither will they. I can never get past those words of Dostoyevsky when he made the youngest of the brothers Karamazov say that just one smile, one kind word, may have been the means of redeeming a person's life.

The church is interested tremendously in lots of people. I sent word to a boy the other day, and he came down. I thought it best to talk to him in the study. I said, "So-and-so, the church is interested in you. Do you know that the path, the road that you are following right now is going to land you in Greendale?" Well, he said, "I don't like to go to school." "Yes," I said, "but if you go to Greendale, you'll like it less than going to school." And then I told

79

him about another boy that I had met on the street the other day, a young man; and I said, "That young man was just in the same situation as you are when he was a boy. But he told me that he was buying a house and of his family and of the work. Fifteen years ago that boy needed the help of the church and got it — the kindness and the sympathy and the love of the people in this church." I said to the lad the other day, "you can do it, because the church is interested in you. The people are loving you, definitely." He looked at me and he said, "I'll try." And I said, "Well, I'll help you try."

Blessed are those that are compassionate. So you see the church is that organization in your life to help you channel your compassion. Don't go away from here and say that I say it doesn't make any difference what you do, that you'll go to heaven after all. You see, that's a very limited view. You may not work into the final state of where you belong for a long time.

I have very little concern about the future life. I believe in it, I look forward to it; but here is the place, here is where a man must be saved to live out, live out fully, and the mercy of God is from everlasing to everlasting. If I could only feel that I had the compassion of Christ for all my fellow men, indeed I should be happy. I cannot speak for you, but I can for myself — that I pray to have the compassion of our Lord.

Happy are those that are kind and are disposed to do good, for in turn they shall receive kindness and mercy.

ORDINARY PEOPLE WITH EXTRAORDINARY GOALS

March 19, 1950
Scripture: Hebrews 11:32-12:2

Continuing our meditations on Christianity according to our Lord, more particularly a study of the Beatitudes, we come this morning to the well known one, "Blessed are the pure in heart, for they shall see God." As Christ described one who would be a citizen in His commonwealth, He spoke of mercy and righteousness, of a desire for truth, for meekness; and now for purity of heart. Happy is the man who is pure in heart.

As we analyze that, it would be expressed something like this: Blessed are those who are free from sin, and an overtone in the word means "who are sincere." Blessed are those who are sincere in their purposes and endeavors, for they shall be admitted into that intimate association with God. Happy is the man who is sincere in his purpose and in his endeavor, for he shall be admitted into intimate relationship with God.

All of us realize the implication there of freedom from sin. Happy is the man who is free from sin, who has a singleness of purpose. We recognize, of course, that even in sin, in the definition of the word itself, there is division. The word means "missing the mark." When a man sins, he misses the mark. If an ancient archer strung and drew his bow, and shot the arrow so that it missed the mark, he had failed to coordinate himself physically. Even so when we miss the mark spiritually, we have not been coordinated in our spiritual nature. There has been division, tensions have existed; we have divided minds; we have been drawn this way and that. There has been civil strife within our own nature; and the endeavor of course is to unify these diversities, to bring them into unity of purpose, into singleness of effort. Happy is the man who is enabled to unify his purposes and his objectives into that which is worthwhile, that which is constructive. For by unifying his objectives and centering his affections on God, he is enabled by the expulsive power of a new affection to drive out the evil way in his heart.

Purity of purpose then is essential if one is to see God. That of course drives us back to the matter of purpose and goals. If I am going to center myself on a goal or goals, I must have some idea of what those goals are. It has been said very effectively that a man's psychic life is determined by his goals. If you show me what a man is endeavoring to achieve, I can tell you what kind of a man he is. Our objectives describe us on the march to their accomplishment.

Now people differ not so much intellectually as they do in zeal and determination to reach their goal. Darwin said that long ago. He declared once that men differ much less in their mental ability than in their zeal and determination. You have seen that demonstrated in life. How often we look back and think of men who were our classmates in college or high school. Those that had the best minds have not always achieved the greatest satisfaction in life. It depended not so much on their mental equipment, but upon the determination they had, the zeal they had to achieve. Happy is the man that has singleness of purpose, purity of intention, who is willing to push forward to his end.

Might I illustrate that very briefly. We have many kinds of goals, many objectives before us. Well do I remember when I made the acquaintance of the English novelist De Morgan. Someone brought me a copy of *Joseph Vance* as I lay sick in a French hospital in 1918. I had never read De Morgan before; after that I read all of his novels. In *Joseph Vance* he makes one of his characters say this: I was honor man in the University, but I have not achieved much in life, for I became so interested in chess that I forsook my profession and gave myself unremittently to playing chess and to becoming an expert chess player. But there are men, said he, in England who can defeat me, though I have given my life to it. What was his goal? To become an outstanding chess player. Playing chess is a delightful recreation, but one should be careful of the time.

Many years ago I spent the weekend with a very delightful host up in Westchester County, New York. I was preaching in their church. I asked him about his game of golf. He replied, I have stopped playing golf and now I take the family swimming; for I was a 3-handicap man in golf; that is, he was a very good player; but I found that golf was taking too much time; that if I was going to continue to be a 3-handicap player, my business would suffer. It's a fine thing to play golf and be a good golfer, but if the objective of golf causes your business to suffer, then one must choose between golf and business. And so it is all through life.

What is your goal? Where are you headed? What are you trying to achieve?

One of the great figures in modern English history was that of Cecil Rhodes. Cecil Rhodes had an ideal and a dream. He wanted two things. One was to unify South Africa and to make it an integral part of the British Empire, and the other was to build up Anglo-Saxon relations in the world. Cecil Rhodes recognized that he must be a wealthy man if he did these things; so he gave himself to the acquisition of wealth. He would work a year, return to Oxford for a year, then back to work; so it took him eight years to graduate from Oxford. After that he became one of the fabulously wealthy

83

men of the world, doing it in order to achieve his end; to build up the Union of South Africa and to build up Anglo-Saxon relations in the world. To accomplish the latter he founded the scholarships at Oxford that are called the Rhodes Scholarships. Rhodes fellows go from all the Anglo-Saxon countries in the world to England to study and return to their own countries to build up better relationships among the Anglo-Saxon people.

Cecil Rhodes did not achieve his end fully. Yet he achieved his end in doing what he started to do; and he became wealthy, not in order to have money but in order to implement his dream.

What is your aim? What is your goal? Where are you headed?

Blessed are those, though, that have a singleness of purpose that is spiritual; that achieve ends for God.

I've always been interested in Dwight L. Moody. I heard a story the other day that reminded me of Moody. Moody you know went to Chicago as a young man to work in a shoe store. He was a clerk in a shoe store. He was an exceptionally good clerk. Dwight L. Moody had a drive that would have made him one of the millionaires of that day when millionaires were spreading all over the country. But he was converted. He was brought to a knowledge of God in Christ and recognized his need of Jesus in his life and also in the life of his fellow men. Said Dwight L. Moody, I am going to give myself unreservedly to God to see what God can do with an individual who has surrendered himself absolutely to His call.

You know what Dwight L. Moody did. He was not an educated man; he had not been to college or the university. When he spoke in Oxford University and in Cambridge, the students came to mock; they remained to pray, before the overwhelming conviction and sincerity of the man. His goal was a completely surrendered life to God, and you know what he did with his life.

Now the story that I heard the other day was brought up by a reference to an incident that I referred to in a sermon not long ago and to a book that is to come out shortly. You remember that I told you of the man who had finished his work as a banker and retired, then entered the theological seminary and took the full three-year course and was ordained as a Presbyterian minister at the age of 65. The book that is coming out is called *The Story of a New England Schoolmaster*. There was a young man who graduated from Amherst back in the days when Moody was doing his great work. This young man had a mastery of the French language, but he had a dream that he wanted to be a doctor. Dwight L. Moody met him, and Mr. Moody through that genius that he had laid a mission on that young man. He said, "I want you to be the principal of our boys' school at Mt. Hermon." And this young graduate went to Mt. Hermon and for forty years was the principal of the famous boys' school in New England. Thousands of young men went through that school and entered Dartmouth and Amherst and Williams and Harvard and Yale and Princeton and the colleges of the East. But he still had, back in his mind, this desire to be a doctor.

When he was retired as headmaster at Mt. Hermon at the age of seventy, what did he do? This is what he did. He crossed the seas to Paris and entered the Medical School of Sorbonne University, where he took the four-year medical course and graduated with distinction as a doctor from the Sorbonne at the age of 74. Then he served a year as an intern in a hospital on the Continent and returned to New England when he was 75 years old and began the practice of medicine in a New England township.

What is your ideal? What is your goal? Where are you headed? Is it constructively, or destructively? Is your goal to have a good time? Is it to be like Beau Brummel, who lives because he was the best-dressed man in England? Is it to be known for your entertaining, for your skillful conversations, for your ability to make money? What is your goal or goals? Where are you headed? Happy is the man that has a singleness of purpose, purity of intention; for I tell you my friends, particularly my young friends, decide on that which you want to do with your life. Pick out your goal or goals, and give yourself with great enthusiasm to it. As Darwin said, there is not so much difference in your mental equipment from your fellows; there is tremendous difference in the zeal and determination a person has to make his life.

And that of course brings us to this thought with which I would close, that I am interested primarily in the goal of the Christian life. What kind of a character do I want? Do I develop with this purity of intention to be like the character of our Lord? Have I set before me as my ideal, no matter my vocation, the ideal of being a Christian? If I have, I must give myself to it with complete devotion. I shall be disappointed along the way, of course I will; but if I have that singleness of purpose, I will grow in humility, I will grow in patience, and in longsuffering and in thoughtfulness and in love.

Suppose a person who was a Christian, who had perhaps what we would call a bad temper, quick to anger; suppose that at 55 he was losing his temper and throwing his weight around just as much as he had done at 25. Well, those thirty years, you see, would not have marked growth in Christianity. He had not given himself to it. Am I more patient? Am I more tolerant? Am I more understanding? Here I stand, as I leave my fifties. Do I have more patience? Am I kinder? Am I more tolerant and understanding and thoughtful as I am nearly sixty than I was as a young man at thirty? Well, if I'm not, I have not had this singleness of purpose to build the Christian way.

All of us recognize that we are disappointed along the path, but we keep the goal ever before us. So after all you see, life isn't measured by the amount of money that we make or the reputations that we have, but by this inwardness of ideals and the approximation of these spiritual values.

I've often thought that I should like to have known the shoemaker, the man who mended shoes, who was the great friend and advisor of President Coolidge. Now if a man mends shoes and has a little shoe shop, he's not apt to be in the news very often; but here

is a man who mended shoes, but who had such an integrated personality and soul that he was President Coolidge's closest friend.
And whenever the President was back in that town, he conferred
with the shoemaker. Coolidge, in the eyes of the world, was a far
greater man; but here was a man that had singleness of purpose to
build a character in God's world. And the same applies to our
church as we endeavor to build it.

"Blessed are the pure in heart, for they shall see God."

THE PATHS
OF PEACE

March 26, 1950
Scripture: Ephesians 4:1-16

Continuing our studies of Christianity according to Christ, we come today to that Beatitude which is very present in out thinking in the world, for as we read the daily press, listen to the announcers on the radio, and meditate upon the present condition of the world, there is borne in upon us that we are not living in a time of peace.

Men long for peace as they have done throughout the centuries. You are startled when you read the paper and see that some men say that perhaps we can go another year without a war, or perhaps two years without war, but that we should be on the alert for war at any time. It distresses us. It makes us fearful. We have such keen memories of the recent war and the one of a generation ago, we feel that it would be absolutely devastating to have another war. Yet it is in the air. Men are fearful.

What does Christianity have to say about this? Jesus did not overlook it in His summary of the perfect Christian character. The Beatitude for today, then, is "Blessed are the peacemakers, for they shall be called the children of God."

Before our Lord came, He was described as a peacemaker. He claimed to be one Himself. His followers after His resurrection

88

made the same claim. Any consideration, then, of peace, making peace, must take Christ into consideration. When Isaiah, centuries before He appeared, thrust his thinking forward into a time when One should come to redeem the world, described Him among other things as being the "Prince of Peace." Later on in that same book, when he was describing how we would be justified through suffering, redeemed through sorrow, he said, "The chastisement of our peace is upon Him."

Then again, one of the lesser-known prophets, Zechariah, said, "And He shall speak peace unto the heathen," meaning to all people beside the Jews. Isaiah called Him the Prince of Peace; Zechariah said He shall preach peace unto all people.

When we come to the story of His life, we find it introduced by the same note, a very beautiful story that is told of the Advent season, when the angels sang of the coming of the Babe, with "Peace on earth among men of goodwill." Peace on earth with the coming of the Babe.

Then Jesus lived with His friends, taught, led, in this new way of life that He spoke of as the kingdom, and when He was ready to leave them, He said, "Peace I leave with you. My peace I give unto you." That which He was bequeathing to them was peace.

Then later on Paul, in Ephesians, wrote, "He is our peace." He is our peace. Again in one of his letters he speaks of the "peace of God which passeth all understanding."

There you have it; before and during His life — the Prince of Peace, "my peace I give unto you," "He is our peace" and "the peace of God which passeth all understanding." In the second lesson that was read today, Paul prayed that we should live in this bond of peace, this unity of the spirit. I need not emphasize further then that Jesus Christ had much to say and much was said about him regarding peace. And now in His description of the Christian, these words: "Blessed are the peacemakers, for they shall be called the children of God."

This morning I am not endeavoring to answer any national

or international questions. It could not be done in a sermon; in fact, it cannot be done in any talk or paper. I would suggest to you certain approaches that we could follow if we would play our part as Christians; only two — that which deals with myself, and that which flows into society.

First then, I must have peace myself, if I am going to be a peacemaker; gaining personal peace. The word that is used means "unity, concord." When one has peace, he is unified. When there is peace among men, there is concord. It is a rather interesting thing that there has been a movement in Christianity within these past years called "Unity." It is not a denomination; it is a way of thinking and living. They are Christian people, but apart from the mainstream of denomination. They call their way of life "Unity," a very beautiful word and a more beautiful objective. I feel, however, that unity can be achieved within, say, the Presbyterian Church as well as through a movement called "Unity." But each one of us desires to have this unity of spirit, this inner concord that we call peace.

You and I know that we are distracted by the diversities of our own nature, that we are tossed and driven by the currents of life, by our own inner conflicts; so that instead of having peace, all too often we have discord. What are some of the things that cause civil strife within, tension and lack of peace? Why is it that men and women do not have this serenity and poise that we long for? One need only mention just a few. When you analyze yourself you see that which we call sin. Any shortcoming or mistake breaks the unity of our soul. If one has hatred in his heart, there is no peace. It is a very expensive business, nursing hatred. It destroys the peace of mind that one has. So often we do that.

I was interested the other day in speaking to a group of high school students at the Henry Clay High School on the subject of "Temperance." I was quoting from Henry Drummond about being temperate in speech. You will recall that I have quoted him from this pulpit, when he says that anger is the worst sin of all. Of all the category of sins, anger does more harm. Now I said, "Young people, one must be temperate in drink and eating; but I tell you this: that it is far worse to be angry than to be drunk." I thought I would startle them, and I did. One boy followed me out on the pavement after my talk, a high school boy, and he said, "Dr. Miles, what did you say about anger and drink?" And I quoted it again. Well, he said, "That couldn't be right." I told him to think it over. When one is angry, he does much harm, you see; wars follow anger, murder grows out of anger, lack of peace comes out of anger. And yet people say, Well, after all, I just lost my temper and blew my top and that's that. Well, that is that; but there's much more to it than that. It goes on and on and on. So anger, hatred, breaks down peace.

I well remember the old lady who spoke to me back in the 1920s. She said, "You know, the Yankees burned our barn in Virginia." I grew up where lots of barns and houses had been burned during the war. She added, "A Yankee lieutenant burned our barn, and I hope he's shriveling in hell today." I said, "My dear Mrs. So-and-so, what did you say?" She was about 85 years old; she reiterated, "I hope he's shriveling in hell today." "Oh," I said, "one should be careful" (I was a young man then; I wanted to be polite.) I said, "That's a terrible thing to say." You see what a terrible thing for a woman to have nourished hatred in her heart for forty or fifty years. It destroys peace. So that breaks down our peace; hatred, anger.

There are other things: fear, a sense of futility, self-pity — all of these and many more break down our peace. If you are sorry for yourself, you have no inner peace. If you are worrying, you have no inner peace. If you are fearful, there is no inner peace. All of these things and many more break down peace of mind and soul.

How do we combat this? How do we meet it? I'm not talking from the standpoint of psychology now. I would speak from the standpoint of religion, which is of course sound psychology. Two things I think one should do in all this matter of finding peace. And the first is to discover more about prayer. I have been trying to pray all my life. Some times I feel that I meet with more success than others, as all of us do: but did you ever stop to think what a marvelous thing prayer is? You have to presuppose certain conditions. If you do not believe in God, you cannot believe in prayer. If you believe in God, you can believe in prayer. I believe in God. I believe in prayer, and I recognize sometimes my spirit is not receptive enough to our Lord to let God's word come through to me. Prayer you see is a two-way conversation between God and man, God speaking to man primarily. Man speaking to God, but man must listen for God.

I had it emphasized in my thinking this past week through a most unusual book that I read; a book that I would not agree with in many points but with much of value in it. It was called "I Leap Over The Wall." You remember the psalmist said, "My God, I leap over the wall." Well, that happens to be the motto of the English family, Stanley Baldwin's family; and a niece of Stanley Baldwin, Monica Baldwin, entered a nunnery in 1914, just before the First World War when she was 21 years of age. She stayed a nun for 28 years, through the First World War, through the intervening years down to the Second, down to 1942—cut off from the world completely; a nun, having taken all the vows of a nun, for 28 years. But she was unhappy. She decided that she wanted to leave this order, and through dispensations—which I will not go into— she was freed and walked out of that nunnery in 1942 into a world that had changed immeasurably in 28 years. You read the story, read the book; I'm not promoting it at all, but it's an interesting, helpful book. She's still a Roman Catholic and her views are different from many of mine; but she has a lot to say about prayer.

Whether a person is a Roman Catholic or a Greek Catholic or a Buddhist, a Confucianist or a Mohammedan—I do not care who they are or what they are, in the realm of religion; if they have had experience in prayer, they have something to help me. This separation of one's self from that which is around, withdrawing for even just a few minutes in the day for prayer. How do you think you can start a day with all of the perplexities without a few moments of prayer? How do you think you're going to meet the family at the breakfast table or the classroom or the bank or the store or the farm—how do you think you're going to deal with people hour by hour, and not have your peace disturbed, if you do not pause occasionally (it may be just for fifteen seconds) to separate your heart and mind from that which is around you, and let God pour in His peace? Now, I'm not talking about something theoretical. I am talking about something that I have proved in my own life; that I find peace through prayer. And that is the only place that I have ever been able to find peace that worked.

Which of course leads us to the example of Christ, focusing our attention upon Christ. You see the figure that our Lord employs? That of a family: "Blessed are the peacemakers, for they shall be called the children of God." Think how the unity of a family is destroyed when there is just one person in it who is not at peace.

You know, families should not live together sometimes. If they've tried it over the years and find that they cannot live together in peace, they should get away from one another. One person can destroy the peace of a family, and that's what I meant by anger. One father, through anger, can destroy the morale of children that will go on through seventy years, because he was not at peace with himself. But if we are at peace, said our Lord, we belong to the family of God, the children of God.

A man said long ago, "He that is well ordered and disposed within himself careth not for that which disturbs outside." So I close with this: that first we have our Lord's example as a peacemaker. We wish to build up peace within ourselves. And might I quote from Thomas a Kempis, who lived six hundred years ago? He said this: "He that is in peace is not suspicious of any man; but he that is discontented and troubled is tossed with divers suspicions. He is neither at peace himself not suffereth others to be at peace." And again, "there are some that are neither at peace themselves nor suffer others to be in peace."

What is the trouble between us and Russia? The Russians suspect us of everything. How can we break down their suspicions? That is the part that we must work out. But it's not with the Russians that you and I will deal this week. We cannot hope to have peace with Russia if we cannot have peace among ourselves, and if you are not at peace with yourself, you are going to be suspicious of everybody that you come in contact with. If you have that inner peace, you can live in harmony with all men. "Blessed are the peace-makers, for they shall be called the children of God."

THE MOST STARTLING PARADOX

April 2, 1950
Scripture: Matthew 21:1-11

You may have noticed in these past Sundays, as we have followed the teachings of our Lord and Saviour, Jesus Christ, that in presenting His view of Christianity, first in the Beatitudes and then later to follow in the Lord's Prayer, that we skipped in the natural order the fifth verse of the fifth chapter. I did it purposely, preserving it for Palm Sunday. The beatitude reads as follows: "Blessed are the meek, for they shall inherit the earth."

The other day when I took the news to the paper, I said to the reporter, "Here are the facts about our services on Palm Sunday and the following week. She read the title, "The Most Startling Paradox," then asked me what it was. I quoted the words, "Blessed are the meek, for they shall inherit the earth." Then I looked at her and said, "Do you believe that?" She smiled and glanced around in a general way. Then I went on to say, "Our Lord said it, you know; 'Blessed are the meek, for they shall inherit the earth.'" And her comment was that not many people seemed to practice it, and my reply also was that generally speaking not many people believe that statement, Blessed are the meek; for in daily life it would

95

seem that many other characteristics are emphasized rather than that of meekness when one desires to gain prominence or achieve success or go from strength to strength.

The reason of course that it is natural for Palm Sunday is that the writer of Matthew went back into the Old Testament to the book of Zechariah to give a theme verse, as it were, for the triumphal entry. He reminded his readers that many years before Christ, Zechariah in proclaiming the coming of the Kingdom said, "Rejoice, O daughters of Jerusalem; rejoice, O Zion, for thy King cometh, meek, and riding upon an ass," the colt of a beast of burden. "Rejoice, for thy King cometh, meek, and riding upon a beast of burden." So the writer of Matthew felt that Jesus was demonstrating the words that had been written centuries before.

Now this word of our Lord was not original with Him. He was quoting from the 37th Psalm. If you take your Bibles and read it, you will find that the Psalmist there said this: "The meek shall inherit the earth, and shall delight themselves in the abundance of peace." Many, many centuries before Christ, some writer with great insight into life penned those words: Blessed are the meek, for they "shall inherit the earth and shall delight themselves in the abundance of peace." No one paid much attention to that statement; not many people believed it. In all probability it would have been lost sight of in the many beautiful sayings of the Old Testament if Jesus had not reached back and brought it to light here, placing it in His description of a citizen in God's kingdom.

There are two men in the Bible characterized as being meek, only two of whom the word is used. In the book of Numbers we read that Moses was having a controversy with his brother and sister; or rather Aaron and Miriam were having a controversy with Moses. The writer says that the man Moses was "very meek above all the men which did inhabit the earth." One translation has it, "very devout, very humble." The man Moses was very meek, more so than any man in all the world.

Later on, Jesus, when He was talking about the problems of

life and what He had to offer, uttered a statement that is perhaps the greatest thing that He said in all His ministry: "Come unto me, all ye that labour and are heavy-laden, and I will give you rest. Take my yoke upon you and learn of me, for I am meek and lowly in heart, and ye shall find rest unto your souls." There you have the occurrences of the word as far as people are concerned.

The Psalmist made a general statement; Jesus quoted him. The chronicler of the Book of Numbers described Moses that way; Jesus defined Himself as being meek. Zechariah anticipated the coming of the Conqueror with the same word.

One pauses then naturally to see what it means, to ascertain the truth thereof. That is a problem of course always with Holy Writ, or with any statement that is made about life. It may sound beautiful, it may have great rhythm to it, it may capture our imagination, but the question that we want to know is, Is it true? Is it true? I put before you: Do you believe that Jesus knew whereof He spoke? Do you think Christ was a deluded idealist, that He knew nothing of the actual affairs of life, that he was a dreamer that we follow afar off? Or was He a wise man? Was He from God Himself? Was He of the essence of God, when He said that? Then ask yourself this: Do I believe it? Do I believe any such statement as that, that the meek shall inherit the earth, or is it just a lot of pious talk that can be disregarded at once?

Before you answer that question in the negative, may you look at it very briefly with me this morning. One wants to know the meaning of the word, of course. Used there it has this meaning, of gentleness, of meekness, of humility. Meek is gentle, humble, meek—that's what the Greek word has in its meaning.

Then of course we begin to describe "meek"; we find when one is meek, it does not mean weak. Meekness means mildness of temper; not easily provoked or irritated; patient under injuries; gentle; humble. And when you speak of a person being humble, it means that they are not proud or arrogant.

There is the word then. "Blessed are the meek, "those that

are gentle, humble, not easily irritated or provoked, patient under injuries. That begins to throw more light on the word. Blessed are those that are gentle, humble, patient, controlled, mild, not irritable. We have seen in our previous studies of this matter that the first step in placing one's self right with God and his fellow man is repentance. "Repent ye, for the kingdom of heaven is at hand." Repentance means changing your mind, changing the set of your mind, saying, "I was wrong. I am willing to admit that I was wrong." The problem that we have seen all along is that so many people are not willing to admit that they are wrong. Some people never admit that they are wrong anywhere. Without the admission of error, there can be no repentance. Without repentance, there can be no Christian living.

Humility then is the key that unlocks the gate into the garden of love or into the commonwealth of God. Dr. Ralph Sockman has said somewhere that it is the greatest of all the Christian characteristics, being humble, having a sense of one's own inadequacy, or one's spiritual inadequacy.

Now take these men of whom we speak. When Moses was called by God, he said, I am not able. God told him, you know, he was standing on holy ground; Moses there communing with God proclaimed to God that he did not feel adequate, knowing his own life. But God instilled in him the power, or rather enabled Moses to release the power that he had for his great work. While Isaiah and Jeremiah were not described as being humble, or meek rather, yet when Isaiah had the vision in the Temple and was called of God for his great work, he said, "Woe is me, that I am a man of unclean lips." God rectified that. When Jeremiah, the greatest of all the prophets, was called, he said, "Ah Lord God, I cannot speak. I am but a child." God said, "Before you were born, I had called you, Jeremiah." Moses and Isaiah and Jeremiah were men of humility who sensed their own inadequacy.

Even Jesus Christ Himself had the struggle with Himself and with God, before He had conquered that sense of inadequacy. It is no chance occurrence that John Milton placed the scene of "Paradise Regained" in the wilderness of the temptation; for Paradise was regained when Christ demonstrated to God and to Himself and to the power of evil that He was master of Himself when He left the wilderness. He was a man who had been humbled in spirit, but He knew that He had mastery of Himself.

So humility, repentance, the sense of one's own inadequacy is part of meekness. Then also we have seen that it meant not to be proud or arrogant. We have a saying you know that "Pride goeth before a fall." No generation that has ever lived has had such a demonstration of that fact as we have, you and I. If we go to the field of world affairs rather than our own, we have had two perfect illustrations in our day of the fact that arrogance and pride cannot inherit the earth; for when Mussolini was dangled head down in the city of Milan and his body thrown into the gutter, and when Hitler was killed in a bombproof shelter in Berlin, they showed once and for all that pride and arrogance will not inherit the earth. They thought that it would. They thought that their pride and arrogance of race would sweep all before. They came to an inglorious and an ignominious end.

One of our elders used to love this hymn. He would sing it on many occasions in meetings that he presided over, and it came to me as I was meditating this week on the theme, how very apt it is. Sometimes you know your mind goes back to certain periods in history. Mine lately has been in the Spanish-American War period; a rather strange period right now, fifty-two years ago, because I was reading an interesting novel on the Spanish-American War. And at that time Rudyard Kipling was at the height of his power and fame, and England with its great empire reached out more and more for power. Kipling himself had much to do with the jingoistic spirit of the British. But notice this poem that he wrote; I think it's well to read it over again. If you would care to follow it in the hymnbook, it is Hymn No. 340 in the hymnal:

99

God of our fathers, known of old
Lord of our far-flung battle line,
Beneath whose awful hand we hold
Dominion over palm and pine:
Lord God of hosts, be with us yet,
Lest we forget — lest we forget.

The tumult and the shouting dies;
The captains and the kings depart;
Still stands Thine ancient sacrifice,
An humble and a contrite heart:
Lord God of hosts, be with us yet,
Lest we forget — lest we forget.

Far-called our navies melt away;
On dune and headland sinks the fire;
Lo, all our pomp of yesterday
Is one with Nineveh and Tyre!
Judge of the nations, spare us yet,
Lest we forget — lest we forget.

For heathen heart that puts her trust
In reeking tube and iron shard;
All valiant dust that builds on dust,
And, guarding, calls not Thee to guard;
For frantic boast and foolish word,
Thy mercy on Thy people, Lord.

What Kipling wrote nearly sixty years ago is just as true today as it was then. So you and I must not only have humble and contrite hearts, but we must together see that our nation has an humble and a contrite heart.

May I add one more to it, for we would not have a complete

understanding of it unless I did. We come to that part which says that it's mildness of temper; not easily provoked, patient under injuries. We remind ourselves of the absolute need of self-control in life. The meek man is master of himself, and because he is master himself, he is linked with the power of God. Most of us have this problem of dealing with our own impatience, of dealing with unfairness on the part of others. Humility though gives us the proper perspective. I daresay that Moses thought many times in those forty years in the wilderness the question that the Hebrew hurled at him, "Who made thee to be ruler over us?" You see, I am not ruler over any man. Every man stands on his own. I cannot be proud or arrogant, nor can I afford to be impatient or to lose my temper or to be irritated or to resent injury; for if I do, at this point of impatience, at the point of anger, where I become hurt, I am not at that point the master of myself. I have given way and have broken down my own defenses. No man who is impatient or irritable or angry can inherit the earth because he has thrown away his main defense.

Again periods in history come to mind. This past week several things made me think of Robert E. Lee and of Abraham Lincoln, and then a few weeks ago I heard a man from India speak on modern India. As this Indian spoke, he came back time and again to the life of Mahatma Gandhi, to his policy of non-violence. India achieved its independence, that for which it had longed for many years, not by violence but by Gandhi's policy of non-resistance. I am not a pacifist, yet non-resistance is an irritant to me all the time; that is, to my conscience. How can we find the way to follow our Lord? Gandhi found it, some way. India through passivity broke down the power of the British Empire. Jesus Christ, on the cross, broke down the power of the world. We have Christ for an example; in this age we have Gandhi. Yet I say the path ahead is confusing. But there is the statement, and there are examples that self-control and non-violence inherit the earth.

I said I was thinking of Robert E. Lee. I suppose in our national life he and Lincoln form as fine illustrations of meekness as any men in our history. Washington could be added; Washington, a man of violent temper, who learned to control it; had pride and arrogance, and who controlled it. But this is what I was thinking about Lee; I believe it was some allusion about West Virginia that brought it to my mind.

In 1861, when Virginia seceded from the Union, they called in Robert E. Lee as the head of their armed forces in Virginia. He had been offered the commander-in-chiefship of the Northern Armies. They sent General Lee up to West Virginia. If you've ever ridden over Route 60 from here to Lewisburg and White Sulphur and Covington, you know that rugged country; and there Lee campaigned in the summer and fall of 1861, campaigned rather unsuccessfully. He was called back to Richmond. They said in Richmond, Who is this man that we've heard so much about? He doesn't seem to be such a great leader. Then they sent him to Charleston, South Carolina, to build the defenses and the fortifications at Savannah and Charleston. Later he was ordered back to Virginia. And on a May day in 1862 at the Battle of Seven Pines, because Joseph Johnson, the commanding general, was wounded and taken off the field, Robert E. Lee, was put in command of the Army of Northern Virginia.

Not once in that year had he murmured; from '61 to '62 not a murmur. And then great general that he was, but greater character (for three years people knew that the Confederacy needed a unified command, a commander-in-chief, and that Lee should be the man), he never once complained. It was not until February of '65, when the Confederacy's cause was lost, that Jefferson Davis made Lee commander-in-chief of all the Southern armies. Then when he went to Lexington, Virginia, in the fall of '65, riding into that old Virginia town on his horse, he took over the presidency of Washington College at a salary of $1500 a year. For four years, through the gentleness and the mastery of the humility of the man, he stamped his name higher than he had in war.

Blessed are the humble, the self-controlled, the meek; for they shall inherit the earth. Now, if I have used these illustrations, how can I point it? Just a word as my time is out. Jesus wasn't talking about material things; not inheriting material things. Jesus demonstrated His power through meekness, but the thing is, my friends, that the meek man first inherits himself. Blessed is the man when he is humble, when he is meek; for he gains dominion over himself. He inherits himself, and after a man inherits himself then in conjunction with his fellows who have inherited themselves, they together inherit the earth. Christian people being born again, having God's way in them, having mastered self and being humble and meek, united, will gain the whole world for God and His kingdom. Not today; not tomorrow; but as the Roman centurion said, looking at Jesus on the cross, "This man was a god," we can say that Jesus Christ on the cross demonstrated the power of meekness, for He is winning the world. And only as you and I become meek, can we serve in His army; not of armed soldiers, but of soldiers of the cross.

CHRISTIAN EXPERIENCE THROUGH THE CENTURIES

April 16, 1999
Scripture: Acts 5:29-42

Continuing our studies of Christianity according to Christ, we find that there are two more of the Beatitudes to consider. This morning I shall take the last one, and next week the one that is second in the list.

The one today is perplexing, after a fashion, as most of them are. It drives home the truth that Christianity is no simple matter. It is not something that one can profess merely with his lips or even give intellectual assent to, and expect to live it out. It searches the hearts and minds of men. It is difficult, extremely difficult, to be a Christian. No one ever said that it was an easy matter. I daresay the reason why Christianity has not had more impact in the world during the past two thousand years is at that point—that men have found it too difficult to practice.

You will agree with me when I read the Beatitude that is our text for today. "Blessed are they which are persecuted for righteousness' sake, for theirs is the kingdom of heaven. Blessed are

104

you when men shall revile you, and persecute you, and shall say all manner of evil against you falsely for my sake. Rejoice, and be exceeding glad; for great is your reward in heaven. For so persecuted they the prophets which were before you."

"Blessed are ye, Happy are ye" which are persecuted for righteousness' sake. A rather strange injunction, that a man should be happy if he is persecuted or reviled for any cause whatsoever, whether it is for righteousness' sake or for the sake of anything. We like to be popular; we enjoy the good opinion of our friends and acquaintances. We dislike being reviled. We shrink from criticism, even if it is just. And here Jesus said, Happy are the men that are persecuted for righteousness' sake.

It is a very interesting thing the number of preachers and prophets that have been in jail. One is rather startled when he thinks of that, that throughout the years Christian leaders have been in jails. Jails are no pleasant places. I went down to the court the other day to speak for a young man that was in trouble. I knew that I could not help him, but I wanted his lawyer and his family to know that I was interested. I spent some time there in the court house. I assure you that it was an unhappy experience. Also, when I go to the jail to see anyone, it is an unhappy experience, for when they open the door and let you through and lock it and proceed and open another door and lock that after you, you feel a shrinking within. It is not pleasant to be in jail, even if you are there as a visitor. It is a remarkable thing the number of preachers and prophets that have been in jail, throughout the years. "Happy are ye," said Jesus, "when you are put in jail for my sake."

I wonder if you believe that? Honestly, do you think that's a true statement? Or do you not think that He was just talking to hear Himself talk? After all, did Jesus Christ mean what He said? Is all this just the wanderings of a deluded prophet who perhaps had a slight mental aberration? "Happy are ye when you are put in jail for my sake" — or when you are reviled, when you are persecuted, "for so persecuted they the prophets which were before you."

105

I jotted down just almost indiscriminately some Christian leaders that have been jailed for righteousness' sake. Let me remind you of some of them. Jeremiah was put in jail; not only in jail, but in a dungeon, deep below the surface of the earth, down in the mud and mire. His friends, when he was released, drew him out with a rope. Jeremiah suffered imprisonment for righteousness' sake. A very unpopular man was he because his fellow citizens and fellow countrymen could not hear the truth with equanimity.

The Apostles were put in jail. Peter and James and John; Paul. Tradition is that practically all of the Twelve Apostles were executed; most of them spent some time in jail for righteousness' sake. In the eleventh chapter of Hebrews we read of the great cloud of witnesses who were imprisoned and torn asunder and thrown to wild beasts, because they had faith.

And as you move into modern day, you find that there in Bohemia John Huss was put in jail. (I was interested in a European calling him John "Hoos." Well, whether it's John Hoos or John Huss, you know of whom I speak.) He was imprisoned, then burned at the stake because of his views.

Then John Bunyan spent many years in jail. John Bunyan has been a character that fascinated me throughout all the years. He was a tinker, a laboring man there in England, touched though with genius. When you go to London and see his grave in Bun Hill Fields Cemetery and then walk across the street to the home of John Wesley (we might say that Bunyan was buried here and John Wesley was buried just about where the Security Trust Building is—not far apart): John Wesley, a university man, graduate of Oxford, teacher at Oxford, brilliant writer. John Bunyan, just a tinker, plain working man, but with a touch of genius. They put him in jail, many years in jail for righteousness' sake. While he was there he wrote *Pilgrim's Progress*; the odor of the jail is on that book.

George Fox was put in jail. What splendid people the Quakers are! All of us know some Quakers. We admire them and respect them. Well, they put George Fox in jail, the founder of that movement, because he differed with the authorities. Every one of you that has any Scotch blood in you traces back to the Covenanters. I've never been in Dunfrees' kirkyard in Edinburgh: I hope to some day, where the Scotch Covenanters signed with solemn seal and covenant, signed it with the blood out of their own veins. When they had communion services, they met on the moss hags in the hills of Scotland, and would put armed guards all around so that they could celebrate the Lord's Supper without being molested. The Covenanters, the Scotch-Irish in Northern Ireland; many of them were put in jail, because of righteousness.

Missionaries from the first have been persecuted. Adoniram Judson is a name that rings throughout the world. Did you ever read the story of Adoniram Judson in Burma over a hundred years ago — the years he spent in jail? And in these modern days we've had it in Germany and in Russia and in Spain. Every Protestant minister in Spain has either been killed or put in jail. Today, not two thousand years ago but today, every Protestant minister in Spain is in jail or has been executed.

And of course the crowning illustration: Jesus, Himself. We talked on Good Friday about the cross. When you think of violence, think of Jesus Christ. Think of Stephen being stoned to death by his fellows. Jesus signed this with His own blood.

You see you are in good company. You are in the most excellent company when you are persecuted for righteousness' sake; for whether you are with John Bunyan or George Fox or John Huss or with the Apostles or Covenanters or the Scotch-Irish or with Stephen, Jeremiah, or Christ, you are in excellent company. "Blessed are those that are persecuted for righteousness' sake."

Now in this present day no one is put in jail, or not in America, for religious causes. We had a very beautiful and searching picture in Sunday School this morning. What a marvelous theme it was, of tolerance here in America. A man can worship God in America as he wishes; we fought the last war, and we fought other wars, for that truth. They featured the movie star, Frank Sinatra, to

107

teach the lesson that in America all men can worship God. That's what we fought wars for; that's what we believe in.

Who brought the Statute of Religious Freedom into America? It fascinates me. Two church bodies did it: the Baptists (God bless them) and the Presbyterians (God bless them). Thomas Jefferson wrote the Statute of Religious Freedom in Virginia, but who put the pressure on Thomas Jefferson? Why, the Baptist Convention of Virginia and the Presbyterian Presbytery of Hanover. They didn't split any hairs about whether they had the right to or not. They said to the legislature of Virginia, "We want religious freedom in this state." And when the Congress wrote the Bill of Rights, they put in it religious freedom.

So you and I are not persecuted for worship in America, thank God! If you are a Buddhist, if you are a Buddhist and want to have a Buddhist ceremony in Cheapside this afternoon, you can, as long as you do not interfere with traffic or with the laws of our city. We have tolerance.

But how are we persecuted? We are persecuted in various ways. By criticism, if you will. By being regarded as queer people. By isolation. By being boycotted. By various social and intellectual pressures, a man is persecuted for righteousness' sake. They label a man, they tag a woman, and they put them in a niche and say, They're queer or they're different, and they are persecuted by the pressure of society. "Happy are those that are persecuted for righteousness' sake."

You see then that presents a very difficult problem. If I am to be happy, if I am persecuted for righteousness' sake, I want to know what is right. Certainly I do not want to be persecuted for something that is unrighteous. The crux of the matter is, How am I going to know what is righteous, what is good? One does not have to seek very far. Jesus said, "if you are persecuted for my sake." He clearly defines the terms of the persecution, of the revilement and the humiliation. He puts it exactly where you can see it.

108

But how do I know what Jesus taught? How am I to meet His standard of righteousness? We have His teachings and His life before us. Here is the difficulty, though, that all men face. That is when we speak of the will of God, not to confuse my will with God's will. Sometimes a person says, I am doing this because it is the will of God; but he should stop and say to himself, Hold on a minute. Is it God's will? Is it my will? Who's talking: God, or me? Sometimes we talk so loudly, we make so much noise, you and I, that we cannot hear the still voice of God. We delude ourselves with our own ideas.

So one should give himself unremittingly to seek out the knowledge of God, of the teachings of our Lord. We do it in Bible study; we do it by coming to church; by prayer; by observation. We have many ways to come at this to discover God's will, what is righteousness.

Now again take the question of that which is the core of it all — love. Jesus said, Love your neighbor as you love yourself. Then he further illustrated it by saying your neighbor was the most despised man in your community (because He used the illustration of the Samaritan there). There I have it: God says I am to love the most despised person in my community, as I love myself. In other words, I am to recognize and respect his worth. Very plain. Apparently very simple — but how complicated it is!

So when I am willing to be persecuted for righteousness, if I am willing to be persecuted for loving my neighbor, I must understand what He is talking about. Are you willing, and am I willing, to suffer opprobrium and criticism and neglect and libel, even, by demonstrating to all people the love of God? Or do I shrink from it? I say, after all, I want to be well liked. I'm careful of my reputation. I want to pick and choose the people with whom I associate. I'll never be seen anywhere trying to bring one of God's children into the fold unless they are perfectly proper people. It is amazing how we shrink from public opinion, pressure of public opinion.

109

I need not pursue that further. Just think back into your own lives, how difficult it is. Well then, how far am I to press this matter of living righteously? What is a standard or guide?

The matter of zeal is a difficult one to handle, this matter of being zealous. The question of minorities is difficult. Paul had a word for it. He said, Beware of zeal without knowledge. Beware of those people that have zeal without knowledge. Sometimes the Lord is injured in the house of His friends more than anywhere else. Some people have more zeal than discretion. We have a slang word; I wonder if you'd pardon me if I'd use a slang word in the pulpit. We speak of people being "screwballs." Did you ever know a screwball? It's a very suggestive kind of a word. Well, screwballs sometimes muddy the waters. They go off on tangents. They barge ahead too rapidly, they go into excesses. They have zeal without knowledge.

There are people who are very zealous for Christ who have very little knowledge of the background of the Bible, the teachings of the Bible. There are people for instance who feel that after all, Christ's followers have narrowed down to a very small number. If you say "Abracadabra" as I do and go through certain motions as I do, observe certain symbols as I do, you're all right; but if you do not, you're outside the pale, and you're lost. That's one of the things; they have zeal without knowledge.

First, in this matter of how far we will go, we want knowledge with zeal. There's lots of difference between zeal without knowledge and knowledge with zeal in God's kingdom. So that's what we want to follow as we go ahead with the knowledge that is at our disposal, but with zeal.

Now it is necessary in life to have opposition. No one should ever shrink from opposition. It would be a terrible thing for our country if there were only one political party. It would be unfortunate in a community if everyone thought alike. There seems to be in human nature the need of giving and taking, of opposite views, of adjusting one to another, casting light here and there. So a minority or a person who has knowledge with zeal sometimes forms the counter-balance, as it were, in the body politic and in the body social. He may endeavor to go forward; he may even be persecuted, but he has his place. So much so is this recognized that our English friends do this. The Crown, you see, is the government of England, and the prime minister represents the majority in the Parliament. But they have an opposition; an opposition party, and they have an opposition leader; and that opposition leader in the House of Commons is paid a salary by the government. Doesn't that seem strange to pay a man a salary to disagree with you? The reason they do it is to keep the majority in line and not to go to excess. To pay a prime minister, yes; but over here is an opponent, and they pay him a salary so the prime minister will not get "too big for his boots," we say — another slang expression.

And so in life these minorities sometimes must oppose and oppose and oppose, even if they are derided and persecuted, in order to keep the Kingdom moving steadily. But I think really the place we should go is this, if I might paraphrase Aristotle in his "Golden Mean." On one extreme there is bigotry — people who have absolutely a closed mind; and over here are those who are over-zealous. The bigots and the over-zealous; and the Golden Mean would be those that have Christian understanding, who are willing, as Gamaliel said, to seek for the truth. If we could only remember that: not to be bigots, and not to be over-zealous, but to have Christian understanding. We remember this, that after all, God is true; that there is truth in the world. I cannot break down truth. Gamaliel said, You'd better leave these men alone. After all, if it's evil it will fall, but if it's of God, it will prosper.

I was telling someone recently a story that I may have told you before, of dropping in to see Mr. Chief Justice Vinson three years ago. I had never been in the Supreme Court Building and as I had some time one day I went by. After I got in I thought I'd call on the Chief Justice, who happened to be in. They got me to his chambers after many secretaries and flunkies passed me back. Mr.

Vinson was reading a letter. He said, "Dr. Miles, let me read you this letter." It was evident from the first word it was from a Justice of the Supreme Court to the President. He said the Supreme Court has gone to the "dogs," nobody in the country has any confidence in it any more, there is dissension within its own members, and consequently — he elaborated all these things — consequently I feel that I should resign. Mr. Vinson placed the letter on his desk and looked at me with a twinkle in his eye. "Do you know when that letter was written?" I replied, "No." Well, he said, "It was written in 1849" — just 98 years before I had been there. You see, the same tension.

Now we get terribly concerned at times about things. Be not fearful. God hasn't stopped. Let us be careful if haply we are not working against God. Gamaliel said, Just be calm about this thing; let God work a while. While we press matters, while we stand for our rights, let us at the same time be patient with God.

And the last question as I close. Not only, What is righteousness, and How far must I go, but When to stand. We fight skirmishes in life, and we retire, but at times there will come an issue that we have to stand; an issue of righteousness where we'll have to stand. And nobody can sway us. They brought Luther into the Diet of Worms before the emperor; all the might of the empire was there, and he was just a plain monk who'd been a peasant. The query was put, "Did you write these books?" He said, "Give me a day to look at them." The next day he came back and said, "Yes, I wrote them." Well, they said, "Will you retract?" And Luther, looking at the emperor and the electors of the empire and the dignitaries of the church, replied, "God helping me, I can no other." "I can no other." He stood. You have to stand.

They said to Daniel, All you have to do is just to conform to the king and pray to the king. Daniel said, "I can no other." They put him in a lion's den. There comes a time when one must stand. We understand what righteousness is; we try not to be obnoxious, not to be spiritual screwballs; but there will come a day, and there come times, when we say, God helping me, I can no other.

Blessed are those that are persecuted for righteousness' sake; for so persecuted they the prophets which were before you.

THE KEY TO A BETTER WORLD

May 14, 1950
Scripture: Luke 11:1-13

Continuing our meditations on Christianity according to the Christ, we come today to the second petition in the Lord's Prayer: "Thy kingdom come." That is one of the most searching petitions in the entire prayer. That was the center and keynote of our Lord's earthly teaching, the building of His kingdom in the hearts and lives of men.

At one other place He said, "Say not lo here or lo there, for behold, the kingdom of heaven is within you," and it is translated sometimes, "the kingdom of heaven is among you." He told many stories to illustrate what He meant by the kingdom of heaven.

Later on Paul said that the kingdom of heaven is not meat and drink but righteousness and peace and joy in the Holy Spirit. The kingdom of heaven is not geographical; it is not material. It is enshrined in the hearts and the lives of men. His whole ministry was built around the theme of establishing the kingdom of heaven in life, both here and hereafter.

Now the word "kingdom" confuses us a little because we do not employ that word in our own living. When Jesus was speak-

114

ing it meant a kingdom, a nation, if you will, an order of society under a king. Now we speak of states or commonwealths. In this country, in these United States, there are three of the states that do not call themselves "states," for instance. We speak of the Commonwealth of Virginia, the Commonwealth of Massachusetts, and the Commonwealth of Kentucky. You do not speak of the State of Kentucky or the State of Virginia or the State of Massachusetts, but officially they are designated as commonwealths.

I had an interesting sidelight on this matter of names just the other day. We have been collecting through the years pictures of the ministers of this church. Since 1784 down to the present there have been fifteen ministers of First Church. We have the pictures of twelve of the fifteen. One man we endeavored to locate, Robert Cunningham, who was here from 1806 to 1822. We've never been able to find a picture of Dr. Cunningham, but our good friend Dr. Robert Sanders in Versailles located, not a picture of the minister, but a picture of his grave in Tuscaloosa, Alabama. So he took pictures of it from the four sides of the shaft. On each side there is a Latin inscription; and on one side it said that Dr. Cunningham was pastor for many years of a Presbyterian church in the republic of Georgia. And then on another side it said Dr. Cunningham was pastor of the Presbyterian Church in Lexington, Kentucky, of the republic of Kentucky. In Latin there was no word for "state" as we use it; so he had "republica"; in the "republic of Kentucky."

So whether you say kingdom, commonwealth, nation, state, republic—you know what you mean; an order of society where people live and move and have their being. Jesus said, When you pray, say this: Thy kingdom come. Thy order of society come, wherein Christ, God, is ruler, and men live motivated by the teachings and the life of Jesus Christ.

Now you see that is a rather hazardous prayer to pray. I am struck all the time with the truth of the fact that Christianity is a very difficult matter to handle. It is, as it were, dynamite. Paul called it dynamite. You might use the analogy of an atomic bomb. Chris-

115

tianity is really an atomic bomb. Christ shattered the foundations of the old world. He brought in conceptions of life that were so alien and so strange. He said we're going to have the kind of society in which God is the Ruler and the Father, that all men are His children, and that in this kingdom of heaven on earth, all men are brethren, one of another. And that if you want to know what a citizen is like, read the Beatitudes; and if you want to know the dynamic, driving power in a man's life, pray the Lord's Prayer.

Now I submit to you, it is very strong doctrine; and we take it and handle it very carelessly. We say, This atomic bomb, we'll just pitch it up, and pass it around, and it may drop or it may not. We treat it as if it were a very innocuous milk-and-water kind of teaching, and we say forsooth, we will take it or leave it, as we wish. So you see you have to be very careful when you pray this prayer. I told you two weeks ago that if you ever say "Our Father, which art in heaven," you have committed yourself to the view that all men are your brethren. If you do not believe that all men are your brethren, you dare not pray that petition. If you do not want the order of society that Jesus Christ taught, you dare not pray this second petition.

I say that because it is in front of me all the time. It bothers me, because I realize how inadequately I follow it; how I pray it, and yet all too often I contradict it in my own life. There is no other prayer necessary for life. This Lord's Prayer is all that we need. Such a dangerous prayer. So dangerous that sometimes I feel that after all, I shouldn't endeavor, even attempt to follow it. Every once in a while I say to myself, well after all, why do we have a church? Why do we have organized religion? Why do we attempt to follow these teachings — they are so difficult? Wouldn't it be better just to say, after all, we do not believe it, and we are going blithely on our way and just stop. I tell you, sometimes I feel, after thirty years in the ministry, that it was all wrong, I shouldn't even have attempted to try it. That the church is all wrong. That why should anyone imagine that anything could be built on these teachings of the Christ,

116

for they are so eternally difficult, and they cut so definitely across human nature. They take us where we are, selfish, opinionated, prejudiced people—all of us, you and I—and they cut right across us; and we say, Yes, we believe it. But I say sometimes I wonder if it's even worth trying to practice it.

But then my despondency does not last very long. I recognize the fact that we follow afar off, that we are trying, you and I; but I do not think that we should ever deceive ourselves in the fact that we do it in a very halting manner, that it is so extremely hard to believe in the kingdom of God in this world.

So you see today we pray, "Thy kingdom come" in First Church, Lexington. Thy kingdom come in the pastor of First Church, and in the session, and in the deacons, and in the members. And then Thy kingdom come in Lexington, and in Kentucky, and in the United States, and in the world. But the kingdom must come first for me right here, and for you right there. No use talking about other people. I am not talking now about you; I am talking about myself. Where is the kingdom; how is it going to lodge in me?

In the world today there are two great philosophies, or one philosophy and one religion, that are trying to build a better world. There are the Communists, who say We are trying to build a better world; and there are Christians, who say We are trying to build a better world. We are trying to build the dictatorship of the proletariat on this earth, say the Communists, when all men shall have abundance. The Communists say, We will make you follow our ideals. We will force you to believe this way, and if we cannot force you to believe, we will force you to conform. There are many fallacies in Marxism. There are many fallacies in communism, but the greatest fallacy in communism is this: the belief that you can compel anyone to believe a certain way. It just can't be done, and the Communists will break upon that rock of individuality.

Christians on the other hand say, We are trying to build a better world, and we believe it comes through the regeneration of the individual, through change of heart in the individual. You see you couldn't make me believe anything if I didn't want to , and I couldn't make you. I couldn't force you to. I've always thought of that illustration someone brought about music. We have had a great deal of music in our community the last few days, have just listened to a very beautiful anthem. Suppose I should meet one of you after church today and say, Wasn't that a beautiful anthem? And you would reply, No, I didn't care for that. I would rejoin, But it was a beautiful anthem, and you'd say, No, it wasn't a beautiful anthem. And I would take a hymnbook saying, I will bash you over the head with this hymnbook and make you believe it was a beautiful anthem. Well, I could just absolutely disintegrate the hymnbook on your head with the force of it, but you still wouldn't believe it. You can never force a person to believe anything. Christianity says, You can never force people. It must only be through the change of heart. Communism uses power, and Christianity employs love; therein is the great difference — power and love trying to move men.

Christians say this, that we believe that while we change the individual heart to bring this kingdom of heaven, we recognize that men work together in groups. Therefore we have the church. The individual cannot do much alone, but the church, the union of individuals, can do it. We of the Reformed Church look to John Calvin for our polity and our doctrine; and well we do, great man that he was. John Calvin in Geneva had a church and a church government, church polity and doctrine so that people called it what? Not only the church. The Holy Community. That's what the Calvinistic churches were to start with; a Holy Community. Christian people believing individually, Christian peoples linked together to build their views in the world. That's the only reason we have a church. That's the only excuse for the church, that men may propagate these teachings and may plan for that which is Christlike. When ye pray, said our Lord, pray this: Thy kingdom come. So the church is the organization of individual Christians to build God's

118

kingdom in the world.

Now might I just very hastily add one or two things to that. We enter the kingdom, we become citizens in this commonwealth, through repentance. "Repent ye, for the kingdom of heaven is at hand." We saw some weeks ago that that meant, repentance meant, change of mind; change my mind that I may enter the kingdom of heaven. Change my mind to recognize that I have been wrong, that I have erred, that I have missed the way, that I want to be as Christ.

Of course that is the crux of the whole situation. Are you willing to change you mind? Do you believe that you are right, always? Well, if you're the kind of person that believes that you are right always, you have a very unhappy husband or wife, whichever the case is. Any wife that thinks she is right always, makes for an unhappy home; and any husband who thinks he is right always, makes for an unhappy home. But I know people — seriously now, I know people who never once in their lives admitted that they were wrong. Not one single time did they ever admit that they were wrong. That, you see, is the key to the kingdom. A person says to God, I stop, I admit that I was wrong. It takes a lot of grace, a lot of humility, a lot of patience. How self-centered we are. And I'll tell you a secret. I hate to be put in the wrong. I hate to find that I am wrong. It is no easy matter for me to go to a person and say, Well look here, after all, I made a mistake; I was wrong in that. And if it's hard for me, I expect it's hard for you. Certainly I'm just an average, normal human being. So we say to God, I was wrong: I want you to right me on this.

We develop this inner life through prayer. Every day we pray the Lord's Prayer. Today we are praying, "Thy kingdom come." I think about it all day and all week: "Thy kingdom come." In Lexington, in my life — Thy kingdom come. Only through this prayer can I build up my inner life.

We meditate upon the characteristics of a Christian, these teachings and Beatitudes, this matter of righteousness and love and mercy, of thoughtfulness and kindness. Jesus all the way through did this in life: He emphasized the mistakes of the spirit rather than the mistakes of the flesh. Now He did not condone the mistakes of the flesh; He said they were wrong. But they are more easily understood than the mistakes of the spirit. In other words, if one of you should get drunk this afternoon and be a nuisance to yourself and the community and be arrested, it wouldn't worry me half as much as if one of you were unkind to a fellow being. And I assure you it wouldn't worry your Lord half as much. Christ would much rather you'd get drunk today than that you be unkind. You see after all, in getting drunk, you might have a headache, you might be frustrated, you might be disappointed, you might be disillusioned—any number of things might happen to you and you'd get drunk. But if you are unkind, you may have caused one of God's children unhappiness the rest of his life. Now I hasten to say, Don't go out and say Dr. Miles said get drunk this afternoon. Not at all. But if you were coming to me for help this week, I would feel that you were in much better shape if you had gotten drunk than if you had been unkind. You see what I mean? That's not original with me; that's original with Jesus Christ. I'm quoting Him, not myself.

So you have to have a conviction about this matter of the kingdom. You want to believe in it; you want to believe that there is a way, the way of God, in life.

I had an interesting conversation this week, and I read an interesting story. Let me close with them. We have come today to Mother's Day. Now apart from sentimentality, and it's very easy to be sentimental, what is this reason that we have Mother's Day and Father's Day and Family Day? Because fathers and mothers hold the key to the whole situation of this matter of building the Christian life.

I read the other day that in juvenile courts a rather large percentage of the children—I think some 33 percent—had been in Sunday school and church, but the Sunday school hadn't kept them out of the juvenile court, and the church hadn't. And a much larger percent had not been in Sunday school but had been in school, and the school couldn't keep them out. The contention was, that which kept them out of the juvenile court was a happy home. A loving mother and a loving father, an ordered home. How do we come at this thing? Right at the start at home. When two parents stand up with their baby to be baptized and say, I pledge to rear this child in the fear and admonition of the Lord, we're at the groundwork of the kingdom of heaven, for of such is the kingdom of heaven. Our parents hold the key.

I was talking to a college professor the other day about Sunday school. He remarked, "You know, my children love to go to Sunday school. They just love to go to Sunday school. And someone said to me the other day, 'You might punish them by saying, if you're bad, you'll have to go to Sunday school.' Wasn't that a terrible statement?" said this man. "I do this," said he. "If my little girls begin to get a little obstreperous (and whose little girls do not, as well as boys?), along about Thursday I'll caution, 'If you don't watch your step, if you're not a better girl, I'll not let you go to Sunday school on Sunday.'" See? Well, that may be a bad pedagogy. I do not know. But at least it's a right step that a child loves Sunday school so that it was a great attraction and treat. The parents tremendously concerned in the child's development.

But the story, much more searching than that. I commend it to you. It's in the May number of Harper's magazine. It's called "Full Circle" and it's the kind of story that is must reading for parents. Here was a couple in New York in the publishing business, a sophisticated kind of couple. Their friends were authors and writers and publishers and professional people. They would meet every day in somebody's apartment, theirs or somebody else's, for cocktails and would talk and a lot of them would eat dinner together. Almost everybody would get just a little high, not drunk but just a little high, almost every day.

They had a boy twelve years old. They decided that they

would have to get out of New York in order to have some kind of family life; so they go to one of those towns in northern New Jersey. Then they discovered to their horror that the boy, who was a quiet enough kind of boy, seemed to have no moral principles of right or wrong. His father found him teasing a crippled child. When he remonstrated with him, the boy said, "We do that all the time; it's fun. We just enjoy that." And there was another case where there seemed to be no sense of right or wrong in the child. So the parents began to look into the matter. The father came to this conclusion with his wife, "When you and I were children, our parents took us to Sunday school and church. We got awfully fed up with the church and bored, and we stopped going when we were older. But we were reared as Christians." He said, "This boy of ours is growing up as a pagan. We've never talked about religion, he's never been to Sunday school, he's never been to church, he knows nothing of the Bible, he's never heard any of us talk about spiritual values. He is just growing up as an ungodly person, if you will. No wonder he has no sense of spiritual values."

On Mother's Day we who are parents remember this, the responsibility is ours. Not so much the problem of young people, but a problem of parents. Do we train them in these values, the kingdom of God? And around the table you can do more harm through an unkind attitude toward your fellow man and build into those children attitudes than you ever dream of.

When we pray then, said our Lord, let us pray, "Thy kingdom come." And I trust that I have made you realize that it is a very searching matter and not one that is simple.

A PRAYER OF DISCOVERY

May 21, 1950
Scripture: John 7:10-24

We come today to the third petition in the Lord's Prayer. We have seen that the first three petitions are built around God: "Thy name," "Thy kingdom" and — today — "Thy will." "Thy will be done in earth even as it is in heaven." When we speak of the will of God, we are talking about that which is at the very center of our Christian living; and might I add, our whole philosophy of life.

Jesus made it very plain that He regarded it so. "I came not to do my own will," said He, "but the will of Him that sent me." And again, "My meat is to do the will of Him that sent me." All the way through His teachings He subordinated Himself to God. "He that doeth the will of God will know the doctrine." We learn by doing, we have His plan before us always.

Now the prayer does not read,"Thy will be done" so that we may bear, but that we may do. It is not a passive prayer; it is an active one. Not negative, but positive. We do not pray, "Thy will be done that we may bear." Thy will be done that we may do. All too often, though, people regard it purely as a passive petition. We think in terms of the scene in Gethsemane. I suppose all of you meditate much on that scene because of the beautiful window to your left; where Christ agonized in the Garden, facing His coming

123

death, the sacrifice of His physical strength, the dissipation of His young manhood. As He faced this apparent defeat, He prayed, "Not my will, but Thine, be done." "If it is possible," said He, "let this pass from me. Let this cup be taken away, but not my will. Thine be done."

Thine be done — how? Thine be done through me. Jesus was the necessary medium for the release of the will of God. He wanted to change the way, if possible. But when He saw and understood that there was no other way God's will could be released, He said, "Thy will be done," and He added in His actions, "through me." So that is the prayer we make; Thy will be done today, through me. Through us, in the world.

May we glance ever so briefly at these well known words. If it is not negative, it requires sometimes a reordering of our thought. Jesus said in one place, "It is not the will of God that one of these little ones should perish." Life presents so very many problems. There are questions that confront us every day, all the days, through the days. One becomes puzzled and baffled and perplexed. We cannot answer all the questions. I have never been able to answer all the questions in my own life; nor have I been able to answer the questions of others, completely. Thank God I have been able to answer some. But not all. "Why does this happen to me?" men and women call out day by day.

To realize how true that is, one could, for instance, quote from an article that President Coolidge wrote many years ago. He was telling about the death of one of his boys while they were living in the White House. This lad was playing tennis, you recall, on the White House tennis court, rubbed his heel, which became infected, and the boy died. President Coolidge said in his autobiography that the death of that boy was the price that God exacted of him for the presidency. Nothing could be more fallacious. God did not reach out and touch President Coolidge and take his boy because he was the President.

A mother said to me once that her boy, who's a junior in

college and drowned, had been taken by God in order to punish her. And when I remonstrated with her, she said that I was a very strange minister not to agree. But she was wrong. God does not reach out and take our loved ones to punish us. That is not the will of God. Now in the over-all picture of the purpose of the universe we cannot see, we cannot have all the light; but we know this: that when calamity overtakes us, when sorrow sears our souls, God is ever willing and ready to comfort us. It is not His will that any little one should perish, and the heart of God is touched with sorrow over our loss; and we are bound with Him in a fellowship of suffering and of pain. But it is not just the dispensation of Providence when our loved ones go. Many more things enter into it than that.

So I would remind you that when we pray this petition, we are not uttering a passive, negative statement. "Thy will be done" through me. I came to do the will of God. I am here, said Jesus, to do His will. Follow in His footsteps and in His plan.

Now of course one needs to discover the will of God. If we are to do His will, how are we to understand what it is? The key to it all is in the life of Jesus. Said He, "I came to do His will." Therefore what He did, if we believe in the Christ, what He did was a manifestation of the will of God. I understand God's will through the kind of life that Jesus lived. You see we are driven back all the time to a Christ-centered life. We have a God-centered universe, but Jesus enables us to understand God, to follow His way and to build. That is the reason we study Him, follow Him, endeavor to be like Him; because we believe that what He did manifests the will of God.

When I talk then about the will of God I must be very careful not to confuse God's will with my own. Sometimes we can utter very pious statements; sometimes we can be ever so religious yet be misguided. People burned others at the stake because they thought it was the will of God. They have persecuted men and women because they thought it was the will of God. Even today,

125

this year 1950, people can be persecuted by others because they confuse their will with the will of God. So one wants to discover what this is.

May I spend a few minutes then with you endeavoring to find out something about the will of God for my life? First I think I must realize, apart from Christ, that I am living in an ordered world. I live in a universe that has order in it. So often I refer to the pictures that we see downstairs on Sunday morning. We had a very beautiful one today. And as we looked at Yellowstone Park, I for one felt that here again was a manifestation of the matchless beauty and order of our world. There are things in our world that seem to be contrary to order. I daresay though that scientists explain to us that everything has its place and purpose.

They tell me that we had jet planes flying over Lexington yesterday. I suppose I am a good illustration of either an absented-minded professor or preacher. When I went downtown for a minute yesterday, I saw a crowd on Main Street. I said to myself, I wonder what circus is in town today? I hadn't heard anything about a circus and I hadn't heard about anything special. So last night late somebody told me that it was a special day — Armed Forces Day — and that they had jet planes flying overhead. I didn't see or hear the planes, and I didn't see the parade, I was so busy with my own affairs (and quite a busy day, or week-end, I might assure you). Now concerning these jet planes: men have discovered the laws of physics and chemistry in such a way that they have been enabled to harness nature and fly these planes at tremendous speeds. The laws have been there always; the possibilities have been there always, but men are catching up with God, as it were. I live in a world of law and of order and I try to follow it. And if there is physical law that is ordered, there is also moral law in the universe that is ordered.

The other day we received from the publisher a large book, must have weighed four or five pounds: "Introduction to Economics," by a kinsman of mine. So I started to read this "Introduction to Economics." Very scholarly, very learned book. There are economic laws in the world. But the trouble is that men have never been able to discover and apply all of those laws. If men mastered and practiced the laws of economics, there would be no depressions, there would be no business cycles, there would be no poverty, there would be no want. If the human mind can ever discover the laws of economics and practice them! Learned men are trying all the time to make economics an exact science so that we will dispel want from the world.

You see there should not be a single poor family in Lexington. There should not be a single person in Lexington today who might be hungry, with all the production that we have and all the resources. But men have muddied the moral and economic and spiritual laws. The will of God is that no one should want. But men have not been able yet to think through these laws to the place where they can understand and practice them. So in doing the will of God we are trying to discover the basic fundamental precepts in the world and apply them.

You take the realm of any moral precept. There is a right and a wrong. But there are always many sides to a question. Never think that there is just one side to a question. So if people who have differences would sit down and prayerfully talk them through, what progress would be made. If nations would sit down and talk them through prayerfully, what progress would be made in discovering the will of God.

I listened to four foreign students at the University the other day — a boy from Holland and a boy from Japan; a girl from Norway and a girl from China. One yellow race, another yellow race, two Europeans; very keen, very brilliant students they were. And all of us who listened to them, I am quite certain, felt that here in a microscopic way, was a demonstration of how nations can live together if they will only follow the will of God.

If I am going to do God's will, it is requisite that I place myself at His disposal, endeavoring to follow the Christ; which leads me to say that I must use my equipment. What are you doing with your equipment to build up God's way in the world?

Friday there stood in this pulpit, where I am standing now, a woman that made a profound impression on me and also on all who heard her. She was a product of what we call the "capitalistic system." Her father was a wealthy businessman. Her husband is a man of great wealth. He was president of the United States Chamber of Commerce. Here was a woman born in wealth, reared in wealth, always accustomed to wealth. What has she done? Why, Mrs. Sibley has given herself to building God's will in her own life and in the world. She has six children; she has sixteen grandchildren; she led a normal home life. But the gifts that she has — intellectual, spiritual, economic — she has poured out in the service of God and her fellow man. In Germany, behind the iron curtain, representing the Protestant women of America. In Japan, representing the Protestant women of America; talking to the Japanese empress for an hour and forty minutes about the women of America and the Christian way. In other words, Mrs. Sibley did not take her fortune and say, "I am going to live a life of ease and luxury alone." Certainly she has everything; certainly she has lived a pleasant life; but also she has said, "Thy will be done through me." And when she was introduced that day, the presiding officer said, "It has been said that when you hear Mrs. Sibley speak, you'll never be the same again." And I can say that when a woman like that speaks, you'll never be the same again.

"Thy will be done" — through me. That should be the prayer of each of us.

I think that we should go one step further e'er I cease. This very practical matter, this of discovering the will of God in one's own life, and what am I going to do at a given point to understand what is the will of God? We have a doctrine in our theology; very challenging, very puzzling one. We call it "predestination." I'm not going to preach a sermon on predestination; "election," as it is officially called. All the churches in the world, nearly, believe in predestination as part of their doctrine. There are a few exceptions, but not many. If you want the most concrete and concise definition of the doctrine of predestination, go across to Christ Church, ask one of your friends to let you have a prayer book, the Episcopal Prayer Book. The 17th Article of the 39 Articles is their definition of predestination; much more ironclad than anything in the Presbyterian Confession. Why have we had it linked to us more than anybody else? Well, "Presbyterianism" and "predestination" sound a little alike; that's one reason. The Baptists are as predestinarian as we are, and so are the Episcopalians. So you see we have good company; "the glorious company of the apostles."

It's not a closed doctrine; but we believe that there is purpose in this universe; that the world is moving toward a divine consummation; that I am part of this over-all plan. I do not mean in each particular. It does not matter to God whether I go home one way or another today. That doesn't enter into it; not that kind of thing, but the over-all purposes. And so when I come to make a decision, what do I say? Let me find what light I have. Where have I been predestined? Well, I've been predestined this way. I was born the last decade of the nineteenth century, and nobody asked me whether I wanted to be born on the 5th of October, 1890. Nobody consulted me. I was born that day. I was born in a certain era of the world's history; the Late Victorian era. Nobody asked me when I wanted to be born. And I was of the white race, and nobody asked me about that. Or my sex—that I was a boy, not a girl. And nobody asked me about my parents and my grandparents. And furthermore, no one asked me about my I.Q.—my intellectual quota. Here I was put down in the world the 5th of October, 1890; white child, of white parents, of grandparents that went back to a certain Scotch-Irish background, with a certain intellectual quota. God said to me, Here you are. What are you going to do with it? I am the product of my heredity and of my environment, plus what I did with those forces.

So you see I examine everything as God has led me to this

point, and then I look back and see how it all converges, and the next step I make in the light of the past, with prayer. The other day I was reading in *The New Yorker* (may I say, a very excellent magazine for you to read at times) an interview with Hemingway, who is considered the greatest living American novelist. Hemingway might be surprised to find himself quoted in church; he's not exactly a church writer. But he was saying, of all the men that he had modeled himself after that there was one who was his master. He said (to use an expression of the prize ring), "I can fight them all except one. Tolstoy. I can never reach Tolstoy." And in that marvelous novel, "War and Peace," at the very end Tolstoy talks about free will and necessity. And he said that when Napoleon entered Russia in the Russian campaign, he was the same brilliant military man, had the same marshals, great armies, but time after time after time he made mistakes that he had never made before. Now, said Tolstoy, when you are faced up against a thing you feel it is free will. But when you get away from it, you see that it was necessity; that there is an over-all plan in life. You choose freely today, but fifty years from now you say, well after all, it was necessity.

How did you happen to do certain things? You try to align yourself with your capacities and your equipment, to do the will of God. And the will of God is good and pure and purposeful; and my life is successful as I adjust myself to Him. So when we pray it, we are praying ever a prayer of discovery: "Thy will be done, through me."

SPIRITUAL PROCRASTINA- TION

June 4, 1950
Scripture: Matthew 6:14-21

We come today to the fifth petition in the Lord's Prayer. We have seen that the first three dealt with reverence, and the desire to further God's Kingdom, and His will. Then in the fourth petition we prayed for peace of mind: "Give us this day our daily bread," or as we have rendered it in one translation, "Give us today our bread for tomorrow." The fifth petition deals with sin; the wrongdoing in life. "Forgive us our debts as we forgive our debtors."

Nineteen years ago this month I had the pleasure of attending a great convention in the city of Vienna, Austria. On the way across the Atlantic in the steamer that I traveled on, a group of Rotarians held a meeting. In fact, they had several meetings on the way, and to my surprise, in the last one the chairman asked me to pray. I stood where I was and prayed, not having been warned beforehand. Two weeks after that in Vienna, I was at a garden party given for the convention, a garden party held in the palace grounds of Shonbrun. Some 5000 people at tables in that very beautiful garden. At the table with me there was a man and a woman from

131

Columbia, S.C. After I was introduced to them, his wife said, "You are the man that prayed in the meeting on our boat, coming across. I did not know who you were, but I said to my husband when you finished, 'I do not know who that man is, but I know he is a Presbyterian by the way he prays.'" I said, "I hope it wasn't such a long prayer." She replied, "No, but just the turn of thoughts. My husband is a Presbyterian elder, and I recognized it."

Well of course, there is in the training of a Presbyterian minister in his theological background certain turns of expression that show for one who is accustomed to the same theology. But the point that differentiates Presbyterians in praying from most Protestants is the manner in which they pray the Lord's Prayer. Presbyterians pray the Lord's Prayer as it is written in the sixth chapter of Matthew. When they come to the part, "Forgive us our debts," they say, "Forgive us our debts, as we forgive our debtors," and everyone around them says, "Forgive us our trespasses, as we forgive those who trespass against us." It makes for a little awkwardness.

I recall when Bishop Abbott used to preach for me on my vacation from time to time, he'd say, "Now Dr. Miles, do you want us to pray the Lord's Prayer the Presbyterian way or the Episcopal way?" And I'd say, "Well, you'd better do it the Presbyterian way," and the good bishop would so announce.

I mention this because I want to focus your thinking on the phraseology and the slight difference there is in the meaning in the prayer; whether you say "Forgive us our debts" or "Forgive us our trespasses."

First though, this petition asking for forgiveness is based upon a contingency, and that contingency is this: Forgive us our debts, as we forgive. And the lesson today, "If ye forgive not men their trespasses, you may not expect God your Father to forgive yours." So in praying, especially in this prayer, any request for forgiveness from God is based upon our willingness to forgive. It is in a way the Golden Rule in reverse. "Do unto others as ye would have them do unto you." Be forgiven, provided you are willing to forgive.

132

The other day a college student was asking me some questions about Pope's essay on Criticism. One line in that you know: "To err is human, to forgive divine." It has the spark of divinity in it; it is a God-like quality, this willingness to forgive. It is a genuine test of our Christianity. It does not mean necessarily that one is to forgive, if forgiveness is not asked; and yet even when we say that, we believe it goes beyond and a Christian is to forgive even if forgiveness is not asked. And why do I say that? The reason primarily of course is that when Jesus hung on the cross, He said to God in prayer, "Father, forgive them; they know not what they do."

A few years after that, the young deacon Stephen, who had preached with such might and power in Jerusalem, was captured, tried, and executed by the Jews. As he lay upon the ground with the rocks raining on him, he lifted his eyes to heaven and in his last breath said, "Father, forgive them. They know not what they do." Paul standing by, holding the garments of those who slew him, heard that prayer. St. Augustine has said, "Stephen prayed; Paul was converted."

You see then we have precedent for forgiveness, even though it is not asked. Of course we are to ask forgiveness of those that we wrong. If ever you have wronged one, you must pray for forgiveness. Never do the deacons come down for the offering that I am not mindful of the saying of our Lord, that if you go into the temple to offer sacrifice and there remember that thou hast wronged thy brother, leave there thy sacrifice, go and make restitution, and return and offer your sacrifice.

Today, if any of us have wronged our brethren, we should attempt to make restitution ere the day is done. But to come back a moment to this other. It is difficult to forgive. "Forgive us our debts as we forgive our debtors." Do not let anyone tell you it is not difficult to forgive. I wonder if you have noticed as we have studied Christianity according to Christ how extremely hard many of these sayings are. No simple matter to be a Christian. No easy undertaking. One does not accomplish Christianity by skating on the

133

surface of life. There may be in this sanctuary now someone that holds hatred in his heart, or her heart, toward a fellow being. That person may have wronged you. They may have asked forgiveness, or they may not have asked forgiveness. But you know that it is a difficult thing to root out of your heart this cancer of hatred or unkindness.

Yet Jesus said, "When you pray, ask God, 'Forgive us our debts, as we forgive our debtors.'" No forgiveness on our part, God cannot forgive us. We close the door between us and Him.

So much for the preface, as it were, of this petition. Now a word as to "debts." In St. Luke he called it sin: "Forgive us our sin, as we forgive those who sin against us." And the word *sin* means "missing the mark." It is a word that suggests that you fail of your objective. You take a rifle and shoot at a mark and you miss it. A boy takes a basketball and throws for a goal and he misses it—a basketball sin. And so on. "Missing the mark" is sinning; and Luke said, "Forgive us our sins." But here it is "Forgive us our debts." Later on, "As we have forgiven our trespasses."

You might be interested to know how this matter of the duality of the prayer entered in. The Book of Common Prayer in England, the prayerbook of Edward VI, came into common usage in the Anglican Church before the King James Version. Those who translated the manuscripts for the prayerbook of Edward VI used different manuscripts in part from the translators of the King James and they in the prayerbook of Edward VI translated it "trespasses." Later on, a half century later, when the King James Version was issued with the word "debts," the Anglican version had already used "trespasses" so long that it became the model for public services in the English-speaking world. But the Genevan Church and Scotch Church followed the King James.

Now as it is used here, the word "debt" is that which is used in money matters. A debt is something that is owed. If a man is indebted to you for money, he owes you money. As long as he owes you the money, it is an omission. You have not the money.

134

"Forgive us the sins of omission." "We have done those things that we ought not to have done, and we have left undone the things that we should have done, and there is no saving health in us," says the prayerbook of the Anglican Church. We have left undone those things that we ought to have done. This is praying for forgiveness for the sin of "not doing."

There are three kinds of sins mentioned in the Bible. There are the transgressions, the sins of breaking the laws of God. There are the sins of omission, leaving things undone. There are the unconscious sins. "Forgive me for presumptuous sins," says the Psalmist; that means unconscious. "Forgive me for unconscious sinning." And how may I sin unconsciously? Well, I might buy some article of goods that has been made in a sweat shop at starvation wages, and unconsciously when I buy the garment, I sin against my fellow who has striven to make that garment. That kind of sin, unconscious sin, we pray to be forgiven because we are not conscious of the fact that we are doing it.

Now a word about the "trespasses" — the sins of commission. Very briefly may I mention it. As a boy I recall my father in family prayers saying every night that he asked for forgiveness for the sins of commission and of omission. And as a boy those words dwelt in my mind, but I did not think about them much, the sins of commission and of omission. Well, trespasses are the sins of commission. Here I am missing the mark; and where do I get a standard or norm to follow? Take for instance the Ten Commandments. That was worked out of the experience of the race with God; the ten words of Moses. And the last five deal particularly with sins and trespasses. I am to respect my neighbor's life, family, good name; I am not to covet his possessions. We have then a norm.

We have all through the Bible statements about wrongdoing that we are to guard against. Paul, in the first chapter of Romans, made quite a list. I jotted some of them down, that we are to be careful not to do. Lust, covetousness, maliciousness, envy, murder, deceit, malignity, whisperers, backbiters, haughty, inventive of evil, callous. Those are enough. He links in the same paragraph a thing like being a slanderer with being a murderer. When we begin to look into these trespasses, we find they are very searching.

In that great work that sums it all up and I mention so often or refer to in passing, Dante's *Divine Comedy*, in the Inferno, he tells of the three great sins of pride, lust, avarice. And under those headings you would find every sin of commission—of pride, of lust, and of avarice. To sum it all up, Jeremiah in his prophecy said, "The heart of man is desperately evil." We are to pray to be forgiven for these sins of commission, of the trespasses we commit.

Now Jesus here is speaking of the sins of omission. "Forgive us for the things that we do not." There are two very interesting things that stand out there in my thinking. One is that it's much easier not to sin by doing wrong than it is not to sin by leaving undone. Of course we can draw up a chart and can keep from murdering people, stealing, and committing adultery and being malicious and slandering. You can make out a list, and it's not so difficult to keep. You may have murder in your heart, but I doubt if any of you will ever murder anyone, from now till the time you die. And I doubt if anybody in this group will land in jail for stealing; or that many of you will steal. You can keep those standards rather easily. That's not so difficult. That's the first thing: that the sins of transgression are not the difficult sins to grapple with, primarily.

The second thing that comes to my mind is this: that Jesus was much more concerned about the sins of omission than He was about the sins of commission. Christ was so kind, so understanding. Well did He know what was in man. "Neither do I condemn thee," He said to the woman. Christ had very little in the way of condemnation for the sins of commission. He let us understand that they were wrong; His sympathy developed and His understanding permeated. But when He came to the sins of omission—the sins of not doing—He bore down. Let me illustrate from Him,

136

and then I am through.

I pray now today God will forgive me my debts. Forgive me for the things that I do not do. And therein of course one must exercise kindness and thoughtfulness and imagination and understanding., Let me read you some words from a great parable He uttered:

> Then shall he say also unto them on the left hand (this is a parable about the Final Judgment), Depart from me, ye cursed, into everlasting fire. Repair to the devil and his angels. For I was a-hungered and ye gave me no meat. I was thirsty and ye gave me no drink. I was a stranger, and ye took me not in; naked and ye clothed me not; sick and in prison, and ye visited me not. Then shall they also answer and say, Lord, when saw we thee a-hungered or athirst or a stranger or naked, or sick or in prison and did not minister unto thee? Then shall he answer them saying, Verily I say unto you, inasmuch as ye did it not to one of the least of these, ye did it not to me.

They didn't help feed people who were hungry; had no interest in Europe and China and Lexington. Eat all we want to, but what do we care if other people are hungry? Have so many clothes we do not know what to do with them, but other people may be cold and naked. People can be arrested and go to jail and we say, Well, these are troublous times; we can't be bothered. We go our own way with blinders on, seeing neither to the right nor to the left. We keep the law, yes. We do not steal; we do not murder; we do not commit adultery; we do not slander. We are eminently respectable citizens. But we can't be bothered about other people. We just haven't time or the interest.

Forgive us for the things we leave undone. But just this word as I close. That seems rather dramatic. You do not have many opportunities to meet that situation. But here is a kind of thing that we should bear in mind: dropping a kindly word, being thoughtful and polite. You know I think sometimes I am developing an obsession, strange as it may seem. I have developed an obsession about the social amenities in life. People are careless; they take others for granted. You never know how discouraged a person may be, and you never know even what a thing like saying "That's a nice-looking hat you have on today" or "I heard something nice about you the other day" or "Wouldn't you like to do so-and-so with me? Can't we do this?" or just dropping a note to somebody who sang well or did this well and so on. Great is your reward in the kingdom of heaven.

We leave undone so many things. God have mercy on us, how many things we leave undone. And if we can be alert to it—not be so concerned about not doing things, like murdering people, or committing adultery or stealing (you're not going to do that, not a person here), but be very concerned about kindness, thoughtfulness, understanding, charity, feeding the hungry, clothing the naked, caring for the sick, enveloping within your love all of God's children.

When you pray, say, "Forgive us our debts, even as we forgive our debtors."

TESTING GROUNDS

June 11, 1950
Scripture: Matthew 6:15

We come today to the last petition in the Lord's Prayer, that model of prayer that we have been following now for the past six weeks. We have seen that Jesus taught that men should pray briefly; that they should be definite in their petitions; inclusive in their interests. As He gave this prayer, He demonstrated all of these qualities; for it is brief, it is very definite, it includes all the range of possible petitions. So I trust that as you have thought upon this during the past week, you have gained fresh insight into the meaning and you will be enabled to practice it daily, that it will widen ever in its implications and impact.

Today we have the last petition. In many ways it is the most difficult to understand. "Lead us not into temptation, but deliver us from evil." We shall see that all men are tempted; that we pray not to remain under the domination of temptation, and that we be delivered from the power of evil.

All men are tempted. Let us remind ourselves that there is a difference between temptation and sin. When a man is tempted, it does not mean that he succumbs. When temptations enter our minds, it is not as if we had sinned. One should remember that, always. Even though I may be repetitious, let me remind you again

139

of the incident in the life of our Lord where He demonstrated that.

As His earthly ministry opened, He had an experience that burned itself deep into His consciousness. After He passed through those days, He told His disciples about it. That experience became preserved in the tradition of the early church. It was embodied in the story of Matthew and in Luke. Centuries after that , a great English poet recognized the significance of it. Here we are in the world, you and I, endeavoring to be adjusted, to live the most complete life possible, to be in harmony with God and with our fellow man; to be at peace with ourselves. And as this has been the hope and the ambition of men throughout the years, they have recognized that the perfection of their state was broken at a very definite point. Perfection was broken at the point of evil. Where evil enters into life, paradise is destroyed. We know that. We know it in our own experience; we observe it in the experience of the race. That if it were not for evil in the world, men would not suffer as they do.

With this in mind, the consciousness of the race endeavored to explain it. And in that great story told by the Hebrews who had the keenest sensibility to spiritual values of anyone—in that story told in early Genesis, we have the finger of history and of man's conception of life placed at the proper point: that man has not been enabled to achieve perfection or paradise because of evil.

There is a very beautiful and symbolic story told of Adam and Eve and the serpent, whereby evil came into the world. That story of course does not explain the origin of evil; makes no attempt to do it. No theology has ever been able to explain why sin is in the world. All theology grapples with the fact that sin is in the world. But it has never gone back to the ultimate answer, Why. And paradise was lost. The perfection of man's life is not possible, because of evil.

So when John Milton wrote his great epic poem, one of the greatest instruments ever penned by any man in any language, *Paradise Lost*, he took these scenes in the Garden of Eden, the fall of Adam, the conflict in heaven between the forces of evil and the forces of God. (Parenthetically might we say that so far-reaching has been Milton's influence that most people have their conception of heaven and hell from *Paradise Lost*, though they may never have read a line of it. Very little in the Bible about this, but Milton in his genius painted it on a canvas that was as far as time itself.) So paradise was lost by sin.

Now where was paradise regained? How can we achieve the perfect state? Later in his life when Milton set himself to write that story, he called it *Paradise Regained*. He placed the scene in the wilderness of Judea, the temptation of our Lord. If perfection was lost by sin, perfection can be regained through the conquest of temptation, the mastery of evil. And again we have there a story that one does not break down into each detail, for we lose the impact if we try to analyze it carefully. But we do know this: that Jesus met with temptation. He was tempted at all points as we are, yet without sin, says the writer. And what were the temptations? Three. And as there is nothing to be added to prayer that is not in the Lord's Prayer, so no temptation can befall you or me that was not in the temptation of our Lord. Notice them briefly.

First, the temptation of selfishness. Of using one's own power for one's own advancement. Therein would be included the sins of the flesh, the sins of greed and of avarice. For, said the devil in the story, you are hungry and here are stones. Make the stones into bread so that you may eat. The temptation on the physical plane of life, on the material foundation, as it were. And all of us are tempted that way — the temptations of the flesh, the temptations of avarice, greed, of ambition leaping o'er itself, of striving to put self above everything else. That temptation Jesus met; you and I confront.

The second temptation was in the realm of values. That was this: the devil said to Him, Just leap off the temple now, and you will have safety and you will make such a stir and have such publicity that your campaign, your life's work, will be launched with a flair and a demonstration. The temptation of the short-cut; how insidious it is . That one can gain value without paying the price therefor. One does not gain intellectual strength without studying, discipline and denial. No university student can train his mind unless he is willing to pay the price. We do not continue to have our minds flexible instruments unless we are willing to pay the price. No one builds an edifice that is lasting unless the foundation and walls and all the material that go into it are seasoned and tried. No one builds a character unless he is willing to stay with it throughout the years. We do not gain peace and harmony and serenity and gentleness and thoughtfulness just by wishing to. So often people feel that there are short-cuts to this, and sometimes when the later years catch up with us, we wonder why we are so unhappy and lack such inner peace. We have not built through the years carefully. It takes more than lip profession to Christianity. So the temptation of the short-cut. I would remind all young people here to be on guard against it, and for all of us that is true in life.

The third temptation was the temptation of compromise. Just worship me, said the devil; just acknowledge that I am your overlord, and you may have all the kingdoms of the earth. The temptation of compromising. Sometimes we compromise the best for the good. Sometimes we are willing to forego that which is better for that which is not quite so good. The temptation to compromise. When to stand; when to adjust. What things are of real, permanent value, and what is ephemeral and transitory. That's the question that meets us all the time.

But you see those temptations — putting self first, above everything else; trying to take short cuts in life; not have a sense of values and compromising — all of those, our Lord met and we are confronted with them. So Milton said that paradise was regained when our Lord conquered temptation. At that point let us remind ourselves again that temptation is not sin. If Jesus Christ Himself was tempted, you and I may well know that we shall be tempted. He was not praying then at this point, "Let us not be tempted." For if He were, He was denying His own life. He was not being consistent nor logical. He was uttering that which would have been perfectly meaningless. So the first thing that I would remind you and myself today is that all men are tempted.

But the second point is this: Lead us not into temptation. The use of the word there is "into; remaining, abiding within." "Unless you do so-and-so," said He, "you cannot enter into the Kingdom of Heaven." When you *enter into* the Kingdom of Heaven, you *abide* in the Kingdom of Heaven. That is the way the word is employed. If I go into the Kingdom of Heaven, I am there. I am a citizen; I am a Christian. So if I go into temptation, I abide in temptation. So the prayer is not to keep us from temptation, but to keep us from abiding in temptation. "Lead us not into temptation."

I think little need be said at that point. One should be on guard against nursing temptations along. At times one needs to flee from temptation. One should not expose himself to temptation; he should not toy with the idea of temptation.

It has never been firmly established, I think, whether Aaron Burr planned to set up another kingdom on this continent, and to be a traitor to his country. Certainly, though, from all the evidence it would seem that Burr toyed with the idea. He came down the Ohio and stopped with Blennerhasset. He set up certain machinery there. He stayed in Lexington awhile and made himself most agreeable, and he was in Frankfort and sent out feelers all along the line. He continued down the Mississippi until he found that he must flee. He was captured and taken back east for trial. While he was not condemned — he was freed, evidence is still rather uncertain. He toyed with temptation. He nursed it along. He couldn't quite let it go, his idea of aggrandizement, of being a great man, of not feeling that he was recognized.

I do not suppose that Benedict Arnold meant to betray his country, but he was a man of choleric disposition, very sensitive. He felt that the Continental Congress did not appreciate him; that General Washington did not appreciate him. His wife made many demands for money he couldn't meet. The English played up to

143

him. They sent messages; they said, You will be a general in the British Army. When Benedict Arnold started, he did not mean to be the arch-traitor in our national history, but he toyed with the idea. He nursed it along. He did not make a sharp cut and say, Away from me. He dwelt in temptation; he entered into it and there abode.

So when we pray, we do not ask that we be free from temptation for as temptation is necessary to develop us, you have a hard task before you. And the temptation is "were it not better done as others used to sport with Amaryllis in the shade or in the tangles of Naiera's hair." That is, just to go off and have a pleasant time — that temptation is there, but here is work. We must learn to "scorn delight, and live laborious days." If we toy with our own convenience, we never rise.

I need say no more about that. "Lead us not into temptation," keep us from abiding within temptation. But it's no harm, for instance, that on a beautiful June day and I have work to do and there is a meadow or field that I say to myself, "Would that I could spend today out there rather than working." Now if I can arrange to be there, all right. But if I have work to do, I must work. But it's no sin to be drawn. The sin is to dally within the realm and the shadow of temptation.

He points it up in the second part, "Lead us not into temptation, but deliver us from evil." Praying always that we be delivered from the tyranny and the power of evil.

My friends, all of us have a dual nature. There is an eternal dualism in us. Righteousness pulling one way, and evil the other. Paul said, "O wretched man that I am. When I would do good, evil is with me." Remember this: all people have evil in them, evil tendencies, and all people have good within them. And the evil will drag us down if we do not master it.

I suppose that the older one grows, the more tolerant he becomes; at least he should. We know the foibles of human nature as we grow older. When we are young, everything is black and white. Many shades between, as years mount up. My impression about life is that not many people want to be disagreeable. Not many people choose to be evil above being righteous. But many things enter in. We call them temptations, or we can call it immaturity or maladjustment or what-have-you. And the evil drags them down rather than the good lifts them up. Let us be very tolerant. No matter what anyone does, you can always say to yourself, "There, but for the grace of God, go I."

You may not have a drag that pulls you to drink, but you may have a tendency to slander and gossip. You may not have the urge to gamble away everything that you have, but you may have a disposition that makes it hard for your family to live with you. You may not be oversexed, you may be very cold, but there may be a coldness in your heart toward your fellow man that would be worse than the other. You see, no man is ever in the position to condemn anyone else, for the tug of evil is there, and we should be very understanding when someone fails. Christ teaches us to pray that we may be delivered from this. Not to abide in temptation, not to nurse it along, not to toy with it; to be freed from it, to be freed from the dominion, domination of evil. But even the best of us at times fail.

God Almighty sees the mirror of our minds and our thoughts and our innermost longings, and He is wonderfully kind and patient and understanding. And through His grace and mercy, He draws us to Him.

Let us pray then that we abide not in temptation and succumb not to evil. And that's the prayer. Those words that are added, "For Thine is the kingdom, the power and the glory forever. Amen," they're not in the prayer. They were just tacked on by some scribe long afterwards. The prayer stops, "And lead us not into temptation, but deliver us from evil."

CHRISTIANITY ACCORDING TO PAUL

September 3, 1950
Scripture: Acts 9:1-19

As I come back to the pulpit after an absence of four weeks, I do it with a feeling of pleasure and also of satisfaction in being with my own people again. I heard excellent reports on Mr. Lane's preaching, which is a source of great satisfaction to me and to you also, I know.

Last winter I preached a series of sermons on Christianity according to Christ. Starting today I wish to meditate with you through the coming Sundays on Christianity according to Paul; and while we may not follow that theme each Sunday, it will be our general one for several months to come.

First, Christianity according to Christ; now, Christianity according to Paul. That may seem rather strange at first flush, that one should differentiate between the two teachings. It is not that we draw comparisons, nor that we feel that one is different from the other; but there are different emphases, and it is well that one should have in mind these two approaches as we think and as we live the Christian life. There is no comparison between Jesus Christ and Paul. Jesus Christ, the Son of God our Savior, He who brings us into fullness of life, who gives us the way of salvation, is separate and apart from anyone else. Yet it was necessary in the development of Christianity that Paul should systematize the teachings of our Lord.

I have taken for our theme today the words in this ninth chapter, "But Saul increased the more in strength." He was called Saul as a Hebrew, but his Roman or Gentile name was Paul. Soon after his conversion, men began to call him Paul. He spoke of himself as Paul; so these references to Saul are merely those before his conversion. So might we read, "But Paul increased the more in strength."

When you speak of systematizing the teachings of our Lord, we find one must stop for a moment. Jesus did no writing of his own. He spoke, he healed, he lived and died and rose again; but as far as we know, he never wrote anything that was preserved. After one generation, when the Church had preserved his sayings, had finally embodied them into tradition of the Church, it was highly important that someone should take these teachings of Jesus and put them in systematic form in order that they might be preserved and studied.

I think that we might use this kind of an analogy, though any analogy falls down: that in our own national life we have the great document of the Declaration of Independence, that which was drawn up by Thomas Jefferson and signed by the Continental Congress, that is looked upon as the keystone of our political and religious life in this country. Yet the Declaration of Independence is not complete in itself. Only as it was systematized and documented, as it were, in the Constitution and in the Bill of Rights, did we have something that we could use as a final guide. The Declaration is the essence of our political living; the Constitution is the expression in due form of our political ideals. The teachings of Jesus Christ are requisites and essential for life; the explanations of Paul help us to understand the teachings of Jesus.

So much then by way of introduction. If there were any confusion in your mind about this, I hope it has been allayed.

Today, just a few words about Paul. Something of a character sketch of the man ere we enter into his teachings more fully. He was born in a family that lived in what was known as the Dispersion. After the Jews had been sent into captivity and after they returned from Mesopotamia, they lived scattered all over the Mediterranean world: North Africa, Asia, even back into Assyria and Arabia. Paul was born in such a family in the city of Tarsus in the Roman province of Silesia, north of the Mediterranean Sea, up toward the Taurus mountains. His family was of the tribe of Benjamin, the smallest of the Jewish tribes, one of the most important as far as their contributions were concerned. He always referred to himself as a Benjamite.

Might we remind ourselves there that the Jews had a very interesting custom of keeping their lineage throughout the years. Paul's family no doubt could trace itself back through many, many generations. I have Jewish friends who can trace their ancestry back at least a thousand years; and some of them further than that. They have had great pride in the clan, in the tribe, in the family. It is well for a man to have loyalty to his kin and to those that have gone into the making of his character. It is a bad thing if one worships that type of approach.

Not only was he a Benjamite born in a Roman city of Tarsus, but he said that he was reared after the straitest sect of the Pharisees, that is the strictest sect of the Pharisees. That meant that his people were loyal churchmen, that they were patriotic Jews, that they looked for the coming of Messiah. While the Pharisees have a bad name because of the way they treated our Lord, we must recognize that in the final analysis they were the best people of their day.

Again it is well to pause there. Paul says that "I was reared very strictly." We have erred too much the other way, I think, now; and are not strict enough. Each one of us must know how to keep the balance of life. I referred in my prayer to the golden mean, as far as money is concerned, going back to what Aristotle said.

Aristotle, you know, preached the golden mean of life: Do not take your money and pour it away, be prodigal on the one side; but do not take your money and hug it to your chest, on the other, and be avaricious and mean. There is a golden mean between prodigality and stinginess; and we call that mean "liberality." Well, there is a golden mean between tyranny in the home and absolute license in the home. Somewhere between there is the golden mean, wherein discipline and love and order and purpose prevail, and children and the family have a sense of solidarity and of pride, of achievement and loyalty. Paul says, "I was reared very strictly."

Every once in a while someone will say to me, Well after all, when I was a child I had to go to Sunday School and I had to go to church and I had to do this, and now I'm grown up I just do not want to have anything to do with it. It's just the same way as if someone said, When I was a child I had to go to school and study, and they made me clean my teeth and wash my face, and they made me keep presentable and they made me obey and so on; and now I'm grown, I'm not going to wash my teeth, I'm not going to wash my face, I'm not going to keep my clothes clean; I'm not going to do anything, I'm just going to be absolutely free and careless. That kind of an argument has no basis at all. Christianity is not something that one has forced upon him. It is a way of life. It gives you something to live with and for.

Paul was reared according to the straitest sect of the Pharisees, and I'll tell you this: if you had to choose between a man or a woman who was reared in a family that was too strict or in a family that was too indulgent, you'd choose the strictness every time. Now I say it is better to be between, but I'd rather take my chances with a person that was reared strictly than one who had no discipline at all.

So much for his home and his background. Now a few words about his physical characteristics. What did Paul look like? I noticed in an illustrated magazine the other day a portrait of Napoleon Bonaparte on the British warship that took him to St. Hel-

149

ena. Very famous portrait of Napoleon standing there on the deck leaning up against one of the masts; and it is said by contemporary articles and witnesses that it was a very good likeness of Napoleon at that time. You look at that portrait, you know what Napoleon appeared to his contemporaries. But no one has a picture of Paul. We do not know what he looked like. Renan, the famous French scholar, referred to him as an "ugly little Jew," because Paul himself says somewhere that he was not prepossessing and we know that he was sick a great deal of the time. We do not know. But we do know this: that Paul was handicapped or beset all of his life by a physical infirmity that he referred to as a "thorn in the flesh." We use that expression all the time, "a thorn in the flesh." He had that thorn, and people have speculated. Some think it was malaria, others that it was epilepsy; whatever it was, it was a physical handicap, and Paul says that he prayed repeatedly to have it removed; but after it was not removed, he prayed for strength to carry on.

Now that brings up again as an aside about Paul a very interesting speculation in life about physical conditions. There have been great characters, men and women of tremendous achievement, who had physical handicaps. You need mention only such names as Julius Caesar, who was beset with epilepsy all his life; or Dostoevsky, the great writer, who had epileptic fits all of his life; or a man like Robert Louis Stevenson, who had tuberculosis most of his life and died in his middle forties of a brain tumor; or John Calvin, who died at 55, having been racked by pain all of his life. Or in modern days, Kagawa, who is coming to us this fall, who has been half blind for many years from trachoma contracted in the slums of Kobi.

Those men, and you can multiply by the thousands, have accomplished great things, though physically handicapped. Yet one could not make a rule on that. Think of the men who have had strong physiques who have also accomplished much; men like George Washington or William Gladstone or Albert Schweitzer — all of whom have been blessed with robust health, who were strong physically. So here you have men who were strong physically who accomplished, and men who were weak physically and accomplished. What is the answer there? It's this: not because you are strong physically does it mean you will accomplish; nor that you are weak physically that you will accomplish. But the key is : What kind of a spirit do you have? What kind of an objective and a desire do you have? What are your aims and your ambitions? And when you know that, then you will find the answer in achievement. Paul had a consuming zeal for God's Kingdom; so a mere matter of physical sickness or physical incapacity did not stop him.

I think we should meditate on that all the days. Remember this, that your physical condition should be incidental to that which you do. Certainly we want good health; and if we have it, we should do the best with it. But if we have poor health, what of it? Is it any excuse? Why, we take it as a stimulus.

I am out of my bailiwick in a way, but what do they do to a good horse? They handicap him. More weight on a good horse. Sometimes when you find a person with a physical handicap, it is because they are so good, they've got so much class that they have a handicap in order to exert themselves more. Paul said, I had a thorn in the flesh; and it stayed with him; but he didn't lose. Maybe today you have poor health. There may be some physical condition. What of it? Do you have that desire and that zeal and that drive, that goal? Well, if you have, you can be in the company of Paul and Kagawa and Julius Caesar and Robert Louis Stevenson, and the glorious company of many apostles who have not been defeated by their handicaps.

So much then for these background considerations of Paul. Let me mention a few contrasts in his life that I trust you will keep in mind as we study him. He is a man of rather startling contrasts. He was capable of warm friendship; he drew people to him with cords of iron. But he also made enemies. There were those that opposed him bitterly. He drew men to him; he alienated men because of the strength of his views.

Paul was opinionated. When he had an idea, he held to it, and sometimes he felt estranged toward people because they did not agree. And yet with his opinionated approach, he also was willing to admit his mistakes and to change his mind. You remember that when I preached on the first approach to Christianity according to Christ, it was "Repent ye," change your mind, be willing to change your mind. So Paul had said, you know that John Mark couldn't go with them any more. I'll not have anything to do with that young man, said he. He let us down in the middle of a venture. But later on he saw that John Mark had redeemed himself and also perhaps that he was too hasty; so he called John Mark in again.

Sometimes we make mistakes because we are quick on the trigger and then our pride denies us the privilege of changing our mind, bringing back those whom we have alienated. I have a friend in another city that I have wanted to talk to for some time but have been a little dubious, because this friend got set against another person; and because she got set against another person she is very unhappy and cannot see all around the situation and isn't willing to "back down," as it were. Sometimes we get so far out on a limb, if I may use that expression, that we can't come back and we are ashamed to admit our mistakes. But Paul was big enough to say that he was wrong when he was wrong.

And then Paul had great intellectual equipment, and he fostered the intellectual development of Christianity. We will see that all the way through. He was a man of great intellectual ability, yet at the same time he was a man of emotional nature, of a deep emotional nature. If you want a study in contrasts, read the epistle to the Romans, which is an intellectual treatise if there ever was one in religion; and then turn over and read the thirteenth chapter of I Corinthians, the chapter on Love. While intelligence is there, emotion is there also, very warm emotion. So we have stressed the intellectual side of religion; we must stress also the emotional side.

You know I have been reading manuscripts this summer. I

read much in Kentucky history. I was struck by a statement that John Breckenridge made (the man who's down on the courthouse square, the monument there), when as a young man he went out to Burlington, Iowa, and spent a year and a half there. He wrote to one of his kinsmen about the preachers that he'd heard, some frontier preachers. He said they were very crude, "but I was struck with this," said John Breckenridge, who was then about 21 years of age, "I was struck with the intensity of their feelings and their effectiveness and I came to the conclusion that intellect alone is not enough, but one must add his feelings to it." In other words, emotion sometimes is more effective than intelligence.

Presbyterians sometimes are a little too intellectual and not emotional enough. And where would I start with that? I would start with your minister. I am not given to much emotional display, but I tell you, we need warmth in life, and sometimes we do not add quite enough. Paul had intelligence, but he also had emotional warmth.

He had persecuting zeal; he harried the early Church before he was converted; but he had evangelistic zeal after he was converted. He was a man who was a good writer, but also a good speaker. He was very proud, but he had humility. Great pride, family and intelligence, church; but a very humble man as well. And then he was very practical; he was an organizer, but a personal evangelist. He could organize churches, he had the personal touch, he was a hard-headed, practical man, but also a mystical man. And those two can go together. He could sit down and plan out in a Roman city a church, the building of a church, the organization of a church; and he could have an experience where he said, "I was caught up into the Third Heaven" where he had mystical experiences. It is possible to be practical and also be mystical.

As I close this very brief summary of Paul, I would remind you of this: that in Romans, his greatest book of all, he started off by saying, "I am not ashamed of the gospel of Christ, for it is the power of God unto salvation." That would be the theme all the way through, the gospel of Christ, which is the power of God unto salvation. You and I have come back to a season that we thought we had departed from. Five years ago we felt that the war was over and that as far as we were concerned, people of our generation, war was over. Now we are back, and we are troubled.

Travel about this country and what do you find? Unrest, uncertainty, hysteria, disillusionment, confusion—anywhere you go, whether it is in the national capital or in a state capital or in a small town, people are restless and confused and uncertain; and you and I are. What do we need? We need the gospel of Jesus Christ; not to be ashamed of it, not to let anything stand in its way, but say to ourselves, This good news of Christ is the power of God. We're going to need it. We need it today, and we're going to need it all the days.

So I hope that you and I will find much of stimulus and inspiration and help as we study together Christianity according to Paul.

A BULWARK NEVER FAILING

October 29, 1950
Scripture: Galatians 3:1-11

Today we have a very definite subject. Always on the last Sunday in October ministers in the Protestant churches throughout the word observe what is known as Reformation Day. For it is the Sunday nearest the day in late October in the year 1517 when the monk Martin Luther nailed his 95 Theses on the door of the church in Wittenberg. I am preaching then today on certain aspects of the Protestant Church. The text is the theme of the Protestant Church, the eleventh in the third chapter of Galatians: "The just shall live by faith."

Two words of introduction. First, the Protestant Church is primarily a church of laymen. The laymen, including the men and the women, are the prime movers and those that have the greatest responsibility for the church. First then, Protestantism is a movement of laymen, and not of ministers.

The second thing is to remind you of our attitude toward all other churches. I speak of course as a Reformed minister, one who is in the Calvinistic tradition, one who is trained in the theology of Calvin and in the polity of the Presbyterian Church. Our

155

policy and our attitude is never to be critical of anyone else's faith. One's religious beliefs are a very private and personal matter. It is not in the spirit of Christ to be critical of other men's faith and their beliefs. I remind you often of that conversation that Jesus had with one of His disciples, when John rushed to Him and said, Master, there are men over here who are casting out devils in Thy name, and they do not belong in our group. Forbid them not, said our Lord; he that is not against me is for me.

Within the compass of the Holy Catholic Church, of the ecumenical church if you will, there are all the bodies that we call Protestant; there is the Greek Orthodox Catholic Church; there is the Roman Catholic Church; there are other groups that might not fall in any one of those divisions: all who call God Father and Jesus Lord. We are not to be critical of others, nor are we to dispute with them about their beliefs, nor are we to hold them up in any way as objects of difference or scorn, but we are to worship God as we see and to allow all men to worship God as they desire. And all that we ask is that they have perfect freedom, and that they allow us to have perfect freedom; that we do not criticize them, nor in turn do they criticize us. The Protestant Church believes in the worship of the individual man and woman.

Now while I am on that may I go just a step further, and remind you that we should emphasize those things where we are similar, and de-emphasize or play down our differences. That is true within Protestantism, as well as the cleavage between Protestantism and the Greek Church and the Roman Church. All too often Protestants forget their similarities and play up their differences.

Take for instance the similarities between the Roman Catholic Church and the Protestant Church, or the Presbyterian if you will. We differ very markedly in our attitude toward the authority of the Church and the place of the clergy and of orders and many other things. But there are so many marks of similarity. They believe in God, the Father of our Lord Jesus Christ. They believe in the saving power of Jesus Christ. They believe just as definitely as we do in sin, and original sin. They believe in the providence of God, the over-all working of the predestinarian purposes of God in the world. They have this same personal piety that we have, though they release it through different channels, with which we do not agree always. Here is where you find similarities in people: the hymns they sing and the prayers they utter. When Christian people kneel at the cross of Christ and pray, you find that the differences are removed frequently.

Some sixteen or eighteen months ago I conducted a funeral with a Roman Catholic priest. He and I had the funeral service together. I read the Scripture and had the prayers, and then he had prayers, after which I conducted the commital service. As this Roman Catholic priest and I stood together at the head of the grave, what happened? I read from the Bible, which he believes in, and I prayed and then he prayed; he read his prayers from his missal. And what was interesting there? We had not rehearsed this together. I met him in the cemetery. The phraseology of his prayers was almost exactly the same as my prayers; for after all we were talking to the same God and Father of our Lord Jesus Christ. I prayed out of the great tradition of the Reformed faith, and he prayed out of the tradition of the Roman Catholic faith; but our prayers were almost identical. Now you see we can play up our similarities and we should de-emphasize our differences.

I say this because when I am preaching on the Protestant Church, I am not doing it to criticize somebody else, but I am doing it to remind you and me of our heritage. Marvelous heritage that we have, tremendous responsibilities that are ours. And so I start by reminding you that it is a layman's church; and the glory of Protestantism and the weakness of Protestantism is at that point. The glory, because it is a layman's church, and the weakness, because all too often laymen do not recognize their privilege and their responsibility.

The Protestants look to what source for authority? Not to

the church, but to the Bible. The Protestants base their authority on the Bible, the revealed Word of God. The church is the medium to build the Kingdom, but not the final authority. The Bible is the authority, and beyond that, God's spirit speaking to the individual man. Now of course when one says that, he must recognize at once what the Bible is, where it has authority and where it does not.

The Bible is the story of the great conflict throughout all time between righteousness and sin. It is the story of God's redemptive purpose so that man may master sin. It is the story of the ethical and spiritual development of the human race; and in the realm of the spirit, in the realm of that which is ethical and moral, it is supreme. It has authority, for God has spoken through men's experiences, that they may understand these truths. It does not claim to be a book of history, nor does it claim to be a book of science, nor is it a book of geology or physics or chemistry. It has nothing to do with that. There are parts of the Bible that are very unreal as far as that is concerned. If you were taking a class in anthropology at the University, you would not turn to the first chapter of Genesis to learn about the history of the development of man. That's not what the Bible is for, except to have learned this: that God created man, that God placed His spirit in man, that God recognized from the first that evil was in the world and that there is the question that I am in God's image, that evil is in the world. It has authority on that fact, but not on how man was created, for the writers did not have the information, nor do they have it yet completely. So if a college or university student hears me today, he need not worry because the Bible says that man was created dust out of hand and they tell you that it took a million years to create man. The Bible isn't interested in that. It is interested that man was created in the image of God, and that we have fallen from His image. So in the realm of truth, of spiritual truth, the Bible is the authority, and the Protestants stress that fact.

I need not pursue that further. Now, not only is it authoritative, but it calls then for a study and understanding. Recently I have been meeting with a group of young men studying the Bible; not using any other text book, just studying the Bible. So many of you read the Bible rather superficially when you were children, but you've long since stopped reading. How can you understand the source of authority if you do not know the Bible? Now you see you are Protestants. You believe in the authority of the Bible, as above the authority of the Church. You have the individual right to study the Bible. If you are a conscientious layman you will study the Bible and be informed.

It's just as if a person claimed to be a citizen of the United States and said, I am proud of being a citizen of the United States; and had never read the Declaration of Independence and had never read the Constitution and did not know the Bill of Rights and did not know the Constitution of his own state, and did not know the historical background of our country. Then he stands and claims to be an authority as a citizen when he is completely illiterate or ignorant about the Constitution and the Declaration and the Bill of Rights and the Constitution of his own state. Palpably it's absurd to talk about being an intelligent citizen if you do not know the Constitution; and just as palpably it is absurd to talk about being an effective Christian if you do not know something about the Bible. So the Bible is the source of authority for Protestants.

Now may I hurry on. In the polity or government of the church, it is not a church governed by ministers or clerks. A minister is what? He is presbyter, we believe. I am a presbyter or elder. I am a teaching elder; the lay elders in this church are ruling elders. What does the word "minister" mean? It means one who serves. I am the servant of the First Presbyterian Church. I am not the head of the church. I do not even belong to this church, you see, in the Presbyterian polity; I belong to the presbytery. I am not the ruler, I am not the head. I am the servant—your servant, and your pastor to feed you, but never to tell you what to do. Did you ever hear me tell you what to do, in any realm? Well, if I did, I was slipping that day. You never hear me tell you what to do. You've

159

heard me advise with you and counsel with you, but you've never heard me say, Do as I do, or do this because I say it, or do this for any reason, except as God's Word says it. I am your servant, your minister.

Who controls the church? You do. Who makes up the church? You do, and so do I. We are together, ruling the church, running the church, developing the church. And there is the glory of Protestantism: the individual responsibility in the church. The fact that you, as members, have a part and that the church has no authority over you in any way. The church does not control your soul nor your destiny, but only Almighty God. You share in the running of the church.

From that conception might I say came the great democratic principles of the world. When men began to realize that each man was priceless in the sight of God, that every man answered only to God directly, that every man had right and freedom to voice his views, then democracy was possible. No totalitarianism in the Protestant church, and whenever any bishop in the Protestant Church or any minister endeavors to act as a totalitarian authority, be suspicious of him. If I ever tried to run this church solely on my own authority, that day you should say, We need another servant, for our servant has lost his sense of proportion. But that responsibility is a great one, and if you do not measure up to it the church lags in its efforts.

Then just one other word. Not only the authority of the Bible and the place of the layman; we talk about the individual priesthood of believers. Protestants stress that each individual prays directly to God, and God hearkens to every individual. I wonder if you ever dramatized that in your thinking and living and if you ever really think about it very much. Here in public worship I lead your prayers; you should be praying also. When you leave this sanctuary today, you go out of here as what? A priceless being, far more valuable than this building, or the Coliseum at the University or the Library of Congress or the Capitol at Frankfort or a battleship or anything. You are more priceless than any battleship or any building because you are a child of God, made in His image. And what is your right and your privilege? That you, without anybody else, without me or the church or anybody, can lift your voice to God, your thoughts to God, and know that He listens to you, and He talks back to you.

We have many celebrities come here. I was in Washington this summer, you know, for three weeks, and there are some people in Washington who are important that I could have gone to see, but I didn't try. If I were in London, I might have an audience with King George. But after all, King George and the people in Washington wouldn't be very much interested in me. But God is just as interested in me as He is in anybody else in the world. Did you ever think of that? That here my name, Robert Miles, means as much to God as George the Sixth or anybody; for Jesus Christ died that His Majesty George the Sixth might be saved, and Jesus Christ died that I might be saved, and at the foot of the cross we are equal. I am just as important as anybody in the world, and I tell you while it makes me humble, it fills me with pride.

So I talk directly to God, and He talks directly to me. If God be for us, who can be against us? The genius of Protestantism is, that individuals believing that, go out to do what? To build a better world. So I rejoice in the Protestant faith. It suits my approach. And I am called upon to build His church, not by being critical of anybody else, but by giving myself completely through the channel in which I am. A just man shall live by his faith.

THE MIGHT OF A MINORITY

December 3, 1950
Scripture: Genesis 18:16-33

As I stated in the bulletin this morning, today I am commencing a series of sermons with you that are slightly different from any that I have ever preached. During my years as your minister I have preached from every book in the Bible, some more frequently than others. But through conversations and observation, it has occurred to me that all too often many of us are ignorant about the Bible. That is, we do not have a basic understanding knowledge of the various books contained therein; that it has been a long time since most of us studied the Bible, and during those intervening years we have forgotten much of what we learned.

Furthermore, it has been said (and sometimes with justice) that in spite of careful teaching in Sunday School and in the homes, men and women all too often fail to learn about this basic book. For these and other reasons I plan to preach with you during this coming year sermons based on the various books of the Bible. We will start at Genesis and go through Revelation, a different book each Sunday; a sermon based on the particular book under consideration; and as we can telescope Samuel and Kings and Chronicles, Corinthians and Thessalonians, and Timothy and Peter and John, there will not be sixty-six sermons, but just a few over fifty-five.

Then if you take the sermon the next Sunday as it is mimeographed and keep it for your records, you will have a brief summary of the Bible. I trust this will be a profitable exercise both for you and for me.

Today then we are starting with the book of Genesis. While there are many texts that could be taken therefrom, I want to emphasize in the closing part of my meditation the might of a minority. So the text are those words in the 32nd verse of this chapter, "Peradventure ten shall be found there, and He said (that is, God said), I will not destroy it for ten's sake." I will not destroy Sodom if ten righteous men be found therein.

As we proceed through the Bible, you will find many interesting and stimulating features. You recall that the Shorter Catechism says that the Scriptures principally teach what man is to believe concerning God and what duty God requires of man. Therefore we are on the search for knowledge of God, what man is to believe concerning God. We will find that it is an unfolding, developing revelation; that as the Bible progresses, men had a clearer, wider, larger understanding of God. The Scriptures teach what man is to believe concerning God, and also what duty God requires of man.

The Protestant Church is built on the foundation of the Bible; not the authority of the church, nor of the clergy, nor of councils. The authority of the Protestants is the Bible. Because Protestants neglect all too often the reading and studying of the Bible, they are unfamiliar with the authority back of their belief. They flounder because they have no stay. They drift for they are uncertain in their beliefs. The church has authority based on the authority of the Bible. The final authority in a man's life is that of the truth of the Bible, mediated through God's spirit, touching him as an individual. So much by way of introduction.

The book of Genesis is an astounding one, a very fascinating and exciting kind of book. In the King James' notes it says that it was written by Moses. It was not written fully by Moses, we know, but it is called part of the Law of Moses; for in these first five books he is the dominant character. He was the man that molded and shaped the Jewish conception of a nation. But this book was compiled years after Moses: in the Elizabethan era, so to speak, of the Jewish writing; that is, in the eighth and seventh century before Christ, when the Hebrew writings reached their peak and pinnacle.

I say it is an exciting book, because it deals with infinity and eternity and timelessness, and also with individuals. It is a book that reaches from before time to the end of time. It is called Genesis because it deals with the beginning, and continues through today and all the days. I read it again this past week; that is, I read the whole book in three sittings. There are fifty chapters. I should say that reading the book of Genesis would be similar to reading 125 or 150 pages of a modern novel. It would take you just about that long or perhaps a little longer. I did not time myself, but I should say that I spent two hours in the three sittings reading the book of Genesis, just as a whole, to get the impact and flavor of the book.

May I suggest that you read each book that way? Not just a few chapters or verses, but sit down and read the Bible from an hour to two hours, just as if you were reading a novel or a book of essays or a biography, and get the flavor and the impact and the tone of the book; not broken up in these little verses and chapters as it is in the King James.

Now as you read this book, you recognize at once that it is to be read on different levels. Or perhaps we might put it this way: it was written on different levels of understanding, and the purpose is graduated, so to speak. What do we mean by that? Simply this: You can read this book as just a factual, detailed account of happenings. You can sit down and read it just as if it were a detailed account of everything told therein. Then you go beyond that

164

at once and you read it as a book that is symbolical, of many things beyond the details. Then you read it as types of events and people that are to come, as a detailed story, as a symbolical presentation, as a typical or topical suggestion.

John Calvin liked to use the word "types." He spoke often of things in the Old Testament being "types" — a type of that which was to come. Do not read this critically the first time; just read it for the facts that are given, and then as you meditate upon it, you find that you go far afield from the actual, literal statements. Might I hasten to say this also, that if a person reads this book as a factual, detailed account of certain things and cannot go beyond that, it is valuable. Certain types of minds, certain approaches and attitudes preclude any other kind of perusal. But I feel that most of you would read it in a larger sense than this detailed account of certain things happening.

Take for instance a play like Shakespeare's *Hamlet*. Hamlet, Prince of Denmark, whom Shakespeare resurrected, as it were, from old Danish stories, went back to the Gloomy Dane that lived centuries before Shakespeare's time. He had the basis of these accounts back there of the Prince of Denmark, and he collected them; then with his genius he wrote the play. You read Hamlet on many different levels. You read it just as a play, as these things happening; but if you stop there, Hamlet would not be so commanding. Then you take Hamlet; you recognize in this Prince of Denmark all mankind. You see yourself reflected. His moods are your moods; his indecisions your indecisions. Throughout the play poem you see the symbolism of life; types of life and of people. You could study Hamlet all your life.

An old gentleman whom I heard last winter studied and taught Hamlet for fifty years. When he talked to us about Hamlet, it meant so much more to him than it did to us because he had meditated, studied it all these many years. So you could study Genesis from now until you die; every time there would be more in it than the time before.

165

I have marked four things in the book that I would speak of in passing, then come to one of them for emphasis. There are four basic truths, I feel, in this book. The first is this: that it emphasizes the fact that God created the world. "In the beginning, God." He created the heavens and the earth and the world and all of nature; He created all the animals, then He created man. Now however you read that story, whether literally or as a symbol of the creative power of God, the important thing is to remember that they taught and we believe that God created mankind and the universe; that when He created man, He made him in His own image — not physically, but spiritually. There is within me the spark of divinity; God in breathing His spirit into man made him like He is. There is divinity within us, because we are made in the image of God.

So that which is to be emphasized at first is the creative power of God in the world. Not chance, not mechanistic development, not just hearsay or some haphazard conjunction of all the forces in the world; but there is intelligence and personality and purpose. God created. And there we pause. So that's the first thing in the book of Genesis that I would remind you of.

The second is this: that it deals with the spiritual dualism in the world. There is this dual force or forces in the world and in men. The constant tension and conflict between that which is right and that which is wrong, between righteousness and sin. Genesis introduces the fact that there is evil in the world. How did it come? Well, these men who wrote the book placed their finger unerringly on the cause of evil. The cause of evil in the world is that you and I have the right of choice; freedom of choice. For God said, Here is the Tree of Knowledge. Now if you eat of this tree, you will have understanding, even as I. You will know about the world, and just not live objectively but you will be a part of it. When man, as told in the story, when Adam and Eve took this fruit, they exercised the right of choice. There was no blind determinism back of it, and as they exercised the right of choice, they chose evil in part.

Now it does not explain why God allowed evil to come.

Man has never answered that satisfactorily, except that man would not be tested and tried if he did not have the right of choice. So the second thing to remember is that there is the emphasis on the dualism in life — good and evil — and it runs through all of us. All men have this conflict within their lives, and it spreads out into society and in the world. You will find that in the final book it speaks of Armageddon, the final conclusive conflict between right and wrong; but now we are in the midst of a campaign; the war continues within our lives and within society.

The third thing (and I must hasten on) is that with God the Creator and with His rule in the world that men can take or leave, there is the emphasis on the fact that a remnant will save the world. Not the majority of people, but a minority will preserve the righteous way and will propagate it. How do we know?

Take the story of Noah. Go back and read that story. It really amazed me when I read it this past week; it had been a long time since I read the story of Noah in this summary. But what is the meaning of it? That there will always be a minority of people, that there will be this remnant to preserve righteousness. All the world was evil but one man, and his family. They weren't so righteous at that, but they were the righteous ones. They were saved. Then the story of Lot, and later on in the Bible we find that Elijah said, Everybody has deserted Thee. God replied, There are seven thousand that have not bowed the knee to Baal. And then the remnant came back from captivity and in the New Testament, the Christian minority in the world. "Ye are the salt of the earth," said our Lord. Always a saving remnant in life. That is reflected in the book of Genesis.

Then just one other thing before we return to this minority. There is that great story of Joseph. Jacob and his twelve sons and the favorite son Joseph being sold into Egypt. Again might I suggest that you read that. Very interesting, in the light of modern events, how Joseph functioned. That story illustrates the underlying purpose of God; that there is purpose in His attitudes and work.

This is not a blind world; this is not something that goes by chance. And Joseph, who was sold into slavery, who seemed to be cast off, saved his family; saved Egypt, saved his people, saved, although his brethren thought they were disposing of him. God works slowly, but He works, through the stream of history.

We talk about predestination as a theological term; and determinism in philosophy. It would be very hard, I think, to live in a world that you thought had no purpose or plan, and the necessity of God moves on. So the book starts with the right of free choice. Yes, we have it — free will. And the book ends with the predestinarian conception of God's purpose. And they are both in life. I have free will; there is necessity. I am an individual, and there is God. I can break God's law and wreck my life, but the plan of God moves on relentlessly. Now all of that is in the book of Genesis.

I mention those four things. Now may I come back very briefly to talk about this minority business. You know the story. These angels came to Abraham on their way to Sodom. Sodom, this wicked city. Abraham's nephew Lot lived in Sodom. It says the Lord walked with Abraham — purely a pictorial representation, because the Bible very definitely says God is a spirit. You see how it would use pictorial language. God never walked with anyone because He is a spirit; but this is language of symbolism. God said to Abraham, Now I am going to destroy Sodom because it is so wicked. You heard the lesson; Abraham bargained: Will you save it if there are fifty good men? Yes, said God, if there are fifty. Then Abraham continued to bargain with Him, and he brought it all the way from 50 to 45 to 30 to 20 to 10. Finally God said, I will save Sodom if there are ten righteous men. But there were not ten. There was only one — only one righteous man in Sodom, and his name was Lot. But the problem there was that Lot, the one righteous man, had failed to exercise any influence. He had not lived as he should; he had not made a positive contribution to that community. Perhaps if there had been two men — someone else with whom he could have conferred and lived, worked and planned, he might have been successful. But only one good man, not working at his goodness, could not save that city.

Now this is true all through the Bible, this minority as we saw. The Jews were a minority; the 7000 who had not bowed the knee to Baal; the Jews coming back from captivity; the New Testament Church — always a minority, a remnant if you will saving the situation. That is true in life. That is the way life is, pretty largely. Take in this country. It was a minority that brought our political conceptions to bear. The Founding Fathers were in the minority. They had to plan and educate to get their views across. When George Washington led the Continental armies, they deserted by the hundreds and thousands. A small minority of the Colonists won the Revolutionary War, a small minority of men conceived the Constitution and got it adopted; and from that day to this a minority of citizens take an interest in the nation. Suppose all men and women who could vote would do so. We would change things frequently. It is the minority usually that is zealous and interested and concerned and active.

And what is true of the body politic is true of the Church. I am often staggered with the conception of what we would do in First Church if a majority of the members were really interested; if a majority really worked at their profession of church membership. But it is the minority. Never as many people on the church roll active as those that are inactive; and what is true of First Church is true of practically every church in the world. The minority carries it. Do not be discouraged. Did you ever work on a committee of anything? Almost always just a small number that are interested, and the majority just tag along for the ride. They come along on the impetus of others.

So in religion, in God's work, there has been a minority that has carried it on. But do not be discouraged. The basic text of Calvinism is this (the verse that John Calvin loved above all others): "If God be for us, who can be against us?" With God, somebody said, one man is a majority.

169

One further word as I close. This makes me feel also that in the dualism that is in the individual, righteousness and evil, that whenever there is one single spark of righteousness in a man, that is, when there is a minority vote within his own consciousness, God can take hold of it. I will not destroy that city, said God, if there are ten righteous men. I will not destroy any individual as long as there is one spark of righteousness left within him, for my spirit can take hold of any man, no matter how small in proportion to his whole life and make him into a new man in Christ Jesus.

Will thou destroy the city if there be ten men? I will not, said God, destroy Sodom if ten righteous men are left.

THE INDIVIDUAL EQUATION

December 10, 1950
Scripture: Exodus 3:1-10

We come today to the second of our meditations on the books of the Bible. The one following hard upon Genesis is Exodus. I would remind you that as we study the books of the Bible together I am endeavoring to present in a way a book review and also preach a sermon. Now a book review has the purpose of stimulating the interest of the hearer in the book so that he will have enough information about it to intrigue his interest and enable him, or cause him, to read the book. No book review that is a real review tries to cover all material.

Now a sermon is slightly different from a book review. It is based on some fact in a book of the Bible; it has information, it is instructive, but there is a spiritual and emotional content that goes beyond that of the mere intellect. Therefore when you preach a sermon and make a book review at the same time, you are doing the first in the form of the review; you are adding a spiritual note, or endeavoring to, so that one's soul may be fed.

For a text I am taking the tenth verse of this third chapter; Come now, therefore (this is God speaking to Moses) come now,

171

therefore, I will send thee unto Pharaoh that thou mayest bring forth my people, the children of Israel, out of Egypt. "I will send thee to Pharaoh that thou mayest bring my people, the children of Israel, out of Egypt."

The word "exodus" of course means "a going forth." It is the book of the going forth of the children of Israel out of the land of Egypt. We saw last week that Genesis starts with the beginning of things. It is infinite in it scope, reaching from the thought of the Eternal in the creation of the world down through the creation and the preservation of a minority, into the tribal history of a group of people, the Hebrews, and finally locating or centering on one family of that group, the children of Jacob. As you conclude the reading of Genesis, you find that the Hebrews have gone down into the land of Egypt. There they settled and remained nearly four centuries, growing into a numerous group, numbering some two million people.

Exodus deals with the going forth of those people out of the land of Egypt at the northeastern corner of the Mediterranean Sea, across the wilderness of Sinai, into Palestine, where they established themselves as a nation. It has been a long time since the Hebrews left Egypt. The names of Ramses and other pharaohs have been preserved in mummies and monuments. The culture of Egypt has changed. The power of Egypt has diminished. Yet today that land is central in the efforts of many nations. It is an integral part of modern society. It still plays its part in history. While the Jews have long since left Palestine as a nation, they have recently returned in the republic of Israel. Today in the Promised Land, they are the youngest among the nations of the world.

The geography then of this book is very present. The impact quite real, though the characters have long been dead, and much of the imagery is strange to our modern ears. I read it again this past week, just as I read Genesis the preceding one. I read it in three sittings. I must time myself on these so that I may give you an idea of the length of time it takes. I found it fascinating as always, ever fresh, many things I had forgotten. I realized again that one must read it on different levels, the level of the factual story, and then the level of the overtones and the implications and the symbols; for no one could believe that this book, which was written around 700 B.C. about happenings seven centuries before, could be an exact, literal story of that pilgrimage. Yet the theme and the mood is there, and you go with these people in their trek toward the Promised Land with a feeling of excitement. Not the excitement of a nation, but the excitement of the spiritual transmission throughout the ages of the eternal truth of God.

Now there are three words around which the book is built. We will spend most of our time on one of those words, the other two coming in later in the Pentateuch. But the three words are these: Moses, the Tabernacle, the Law. Moses, the Ten Commandments, and the worship — those three are the central features of this book.

Last week we saw that God works through a minority, that all through the stream of history it has been a minority that carried the load, whether it be in nations, communities, church, club, committee; anything that men endeavor to do, the load is carried by a minority. God has saved the human race through a remnant. But that does not mean that when we are in a minority, when we are a part of a remnant, that our obligation is lessened. Rather it is increased. Here we have the story of a man who was a minority. Sometimes he was a minority of one, in the midst of two million people he stood alone. Again he stood alone in all the land of Egypt against the might of Pharaoh and his court and his people. Moses at times was a minority of one, with God.

I have spoken of those days in the Reformation when Martin Luther stood before the emperor in the Diet of Worms and they said to him, Did you write this book? Is this your teaching? Luther said, I would like a day to study them to see. He came back the next day, and again they asked, Did you write these books? Is this your teaching? Martin Luther, standing before the imperial court, just a lone monk with no prestige, no power, and no support, except his elector, replied, "God helping me, I can no other." In other words, I wrote them, and I stand on my position.

There are times in the world when an individual must stand against everyone, no matter who, if he feels that he is right. So ofttimes Moses was in a minority. But what a minority!

Let us look at his life very briefly as it is brought out in this book; then a word on the Commandments and the Tabernacle. Moses' life falls into three definite divisions of forty years each – a man who lived to be 120 years old, according to the Bible story. The first forty years of his life were those of preparation and seasoning, as it were. You recall the story of how he was born in a Hebrew home and his mother, wishing to save him, put him in the bulrushes in a little basket with his sister standing by so that when he was discovered by the princess, she could come forward and offer his own mother as a nurse. Every child knows that story, a very beautiful narrative. He was reared as the son of an Egyptian princess.

Might I say just by way of parenthesis here that talking about book reviews, I reviewed a book last month written by one of our elders; very able and very brilliant book by Dr. McVey. When I went to the review that day I carried with me a book that I had borrowed ten years ago – not of Dr. McVey but of a presiding officer of the meeting. That's an impolite thing to keep a book ten years, but some people have had mine twenty years and I'll never see them again. The book was called *Moses*, by Sigmund Freud, the great psychoanalyst. Freud holds that Moses was not a Hebrew. Freud, himself a Jew, claims that Moses was not a Hebrew, but an Egyptian, an Egyptian prince who was driven out from the court. However, the Bible says that he was a Hebrew, and the great tradition is that he was a Hebrew. He was reared in the court of Pharaoh, he was trained, in the schools, he became a general in the Egyptian army, according to Josephus, the Hebrew historian. Moses, leading the armies of Egypt against their enemies to the south, was a man of ability in the world of secular events. But there was within him the love of his people, and when he was forty years old he felt the time had come.

Might I pause there to remind the younger people here as well as all of us that life is not an even tempo. One year is not always like another; sometimes a person crowds into thirty years, forty years, far more than others do in a hundred years. Sometimes in five minutes, the whole consummation of one's life takes place, and all else was preparation for those five minutes. Life is not quantitative; it is qualitative always. But be not discouraged. Sometimes the years seem drab and slow, but if you believe in the purpose of God, He will use you in your niche and according to your capacities.

So when he was forty, Moses thought the time had come. He saw an Egyptian persecuting one of the Hebrews, those men who had been made slaves at labor. Moses, glancing around, saw that no one was there and he killed the Egyptian because he was persecuting the Jew. Then Moses, having buried the Egyptian, thought that he could lead them out as a popular leader. But the next day two Hebrews contending together said to Moses, Who made thee ruler over us? We didn't choose you, we didn't ask you to lead us out of this bondage. Moses was fearful. His attempt was abortive. Pharaoh learned of it and he fled, fled across the Nile into the desert far back into the desert of Arabia. There he spent another forty years. Forty years of activity and forty years of the life of a shepherd, tending to the flock of his father-in-law Jethro, going over the land that later he was to follow in leading the children of Israel. Years of meditation and prayer.

Now I think it's well to remind ourselves of the implication of this. You never know when you are going to be stopped suddenly. It may be by ill health, it may be by financial misfortune, it may be from sorrow, it may be some grievous disappointment — you feel that you were ready to burst out into sudden blaze, as said Milton. "When the blind fate with the abhorrent shears" comes it may not necessarily slit the thin-spun line of life but it may stop you.

Years ago I was in a hospital in France during the First World War and time hung heavy on my hands. People brought some books in, and I got possession of William De Morgan's novel, *Joseph Vance*. I had never heard of William De Morgan. I assure you I read everything after that that he wrote. It was a very interesting novel. It helped to while away those hours in winter days, back of Verdun during the First World War. But the point is this: William De Morgan had been a businessman, a manufacturer; and when he was 64 years old he failed in business, due to business conditions over which he had no control, and he was in bed, sick. (Moses now, taken out of Pharaoh's court was precipitated into a desert for 40 years.) What did De Morgan do? He began to scribble on backs of envelopes and pieces of paper, which his wife picked up and put together. Reading them she saw it was worthwhile, and that was the way he started the novel *Joseph Vance*. Between the years of 65 and 80, William De Morgan wrote at least a half dozen novels, the best known of which is *Alice for Short*. He is well known in the field of English letters. Sixty-five years old, in bed, a financial failure, and then he made his reputation. I cannot even remember what his business was, but I'll never forget his books.

So Moses, apparently, was put aside for forty years; but those years were the ones in which he was seasoned, trained, in which he grew in the knowledge of God. Then came his opportunity. God called him at the burning bush, from out the burning bush, to go into the land of Egypt and lead his people out. There followed those years that are described in the book of Exodus.

Just this about those years. I tell you he was a minority. Notice how he was opposed and also how he hesitated. God said, Moses, you are the man. And Moses said, No, I'm not the man. How can I go down and speak to Pharaoh? I'm no speaker.

I always like to think of that story of Stonewall Jackson, when his minister called on him to lead in prayer. He was a deacon in the Presbyterian Church, and he made a pitiful effort. He just stammered and halted all over the place. The minister, Dr. White, was a little embarrassed, but Thomas Jackson went to his minister and said, "I made a failure that time, but you keep on calling on me until I can do this, until I can pray in public."

Moses said, I cannot speak in public. God said, All right, you have a brother, haven't you? We'll send Aaron along to do the speaking. You'll be the leader and we'll have Aaron to speak. He divided the authority. Moses didn't go quite as far that way as he might have, because he didn't trust God. There are people in this church, when asked to do something, are willing to give it a try; but some people say, No, count me out; I cannot do that. I hope all of us will remember Moses. He didn't go quite as far as he might have. He had to have somebody else to do his talking for him.

Here are a few details about his problems. Pharaoh opposed him, and there was that series of the ten plagues. You know if a person read those who was a Christian and who had never read the Old Testament, he would be horrified. That's not Christian writing, the story of the ten plagues. Not at all; but when you read it, you see this: that between the story of the plagues and the story of the Good Samaritan, there are a thousand years, but chiefly there is Jesus Christ who said, "Moses said unto you, Do this-and-so; but I say unto you . . . ." "Moses said, Hate your enemies, but I say, Love them that despitefully use you." You see there is a very definite development in the Bible of the understanding of God and of His love, and nowhere is it pointed up more clearly than in the story of the plagues.

But they finally left, they escaped during the Passover, and were out in the wilderness. Escaped from Egypt, headed toward the Promised Land, and what happened? Why, the people began to murmur. They were hungry; but manna was provided; they were thirsty, and water appeared. But they said to Moses, Why did you bring us out of Egypt? Why did you bring us from the fleshpots of Egypt in order that we would die in the wilderness? Again he was a minority, and again look at human nature. Here they had been oppressed, they had been persecuted, but when they were in a difficult situation, the land of Egypt looked very green. "Why did you bring us from the fleshpots of Egypt to die in the wilderness?"

Every great leader in the history of the world has had conditions like that with which to contend, when people missed the vision. Then when he gave them the Law, the Ten Commandments, and went back for further instructions, they departed from the truth, made the golden calf, and worshipped a golden image. So angry was Moses that he broke the tables of stone. All I say is this, that no matter what you are engaged in, I say no matter what, there are going to be people who fall by the wayside, and we should always watch that we do not do it. There will be murmurings after the fleshpots of Egypt, and there will be worship of the golden calf on the part of people as long as there are people; because everyone cannot catch the vision.

Might I mention briefly four aspects of Moses. First, his humility, his meekness. Here is a very significant thing about Moses, that he is the only man in the Bible that is linked with Jesus Christ in a descriptive word. That fascinates me. There are only two men in all the Bible, both Old and New scriptures, that have one word to tie them, and that word is "meekness." The man Moses was meek above all the men on the face of the earth, says Numbers. And Jesus said, Come after me, for I am meek and lowly of heart and ye shall find rest unto your souls. There they are: Moses and Jesus Christ, described as meek. Nothing weak, no. It doesn't mean weak. It means they were humble. They were men of humility. Because the Christ was humble, because Moses was humble, they had power. There can be no power except through humility. There is in the book of Kings this verse: Let not him that putteth on his armor boast in himself as he that taketh it off. Never boast before you accomplish. Humility — a sense of one's own unworthiness, a sense of one's dependence on God. That is what Moses had. Because he had it, because he had faith, because he had courage, one man as a minority with God led out the children of Israel into the land of promise.

That last word is the quality that sums up his character. He had an ideal, he had an objective. He was to take them into the Promised Land. They were forty years getting there, but always there was the objective ahead of him. You'll never get anywhere unless you have an objective or objectives. There is always that Promised Land beckoning a man, calling him on, making him suffer and endure and have privations. It's always out there, leading us on.

In Leviticus and Numbers we will talk about the Ten Commandants and the Tabernacle. It is necessary to have a law of life, a moral law and rule, summarized in the Ten Commandments; and also essential to have beauty in life and in worship. So in this wilderness they had the tabernacle for the worship of God. Back in those early days, forty years in the wilderness, what did they build? They built as beautiful and lovely a tabernacle as man could wish, that God could desire. It is to me a fascinating thing that all through the history of the Hebrew-Christian faith, emphasis has been placed on beauty and form in worship.

The reason that I have on a Genevan gown, a simple black vestment with my ordination bands, and that Mr. Lane has on his Genevan gown and ordination bands, very simple Presbyterian costume, is because when Calvin broke with the Church, he felt that they had gone too far in ritual, as they had; that no Presbyterian minister would ever be taken for a Roman Catholic priest. John Calvin designed this simple black robe that we wear, called the Genevan gown, so that you would never mistake me or any of us for a Roman priest. But because we have this simplicity of garb does not mean that we are not in the tradition of the garments of the priests and the high priest; and because the tabernacle was beautiful beyond words, it calls for beauty in worship and a church should be as beautiful and as aesthetic as the material means of its members can make it. Back in the wilderness of Sinai, the children of Israel brought gold and silver and fine ornaments for the worship of their God.

The book of Exodus then deals with a man, and with a Law, and with a place of worship and a mode of worship. Said God to Moses, "Come now, therefore, and I will send thee unto Pharaoh, that thou mayest bring forth my people, the children of Israel, out of Egypt." And he went, and he did, and he lives in this book; but far beyond that, he lives in the life of man ever since.

CHRISTMAS BEFORE CHRIST

December 17, 1950
Scripture: Leviticus 19:9-18

When I considered the series that I am preaching with you now on the books of the Bible, it seemed at first glance that I would of necessity turn aside during the Christmas season from these books in order. Yet on second thought, I felt that it would not be necessary to omit any one of them, but to move in sequence through the Christmas season and New Year's. The lesson then today is from Leviticus and next week from Numbers. I am quite certain that it is the first time that I have ever preached a Christmas sermon from Numbers, or a pre-Christmas one from Leviticus. But I trust that you and I shall find that they are apt, that they are fitting for these days and that we shall not in any sense strain the meaning of the books to have the inwardness of the Christmas season.

Today then we come to the third of the books of the Pentateuch or Law, having considered Genesis and Exodus. To-day our message is from Leviticus, the third book in the Bible; and the text that I have chosen is one that has a very familiar ring. It is found in the nineteenth chapter and a part of the seventeenth verse:

181

"Thou shalt love thy neighbor as thyself."

It is called the book of Leviticus because it deals with the sons of Levi, who were the priests of Israel. It is concerned with the Law, with worship and with sacrifice; therefore the book concerning the Levites or the book of Leviticus. Three words stand out in this book, even as three words did in Exodus. They are: the Law, worship, and sacrifice.

You remember the story as it has unfolded — the children of Israel in bondage in Egypt, led out by Moses, the Law-giver. The book of Exodus dealt with that. Now they are in the wilderness between Egypt and Palestine. They lived there a nomadic life for forty years, and in that time they became established more as a coherent group than they had been as a loosely-joined number of families.

We are quite certain that this book carries the imprint of Moses, but received its present form many centuries after Moses; for it could not very well have been written in its present form in the wilderness, covering such a wide range of subjects. There is though at the core of it all the leadership of Moses, the idea of holiness unto God, the perfection of their worship, and the forepointing, as it were, to the Christ in the world.

First then about the Law. In the book of Exodus, we had presented the ten words of Moses that have been known as the Ten Commandments. They are reiterated in Leviticus; but more than that, they are expanded. They have comments made upon them. It is a commentary, if you will, on the Ten Commandments.

Now we have seen so often that this is a world of law, that Nature operates under law, that that which is behind the universe Whom we call God is Intelligence and Personality; that there is no haphazard functioning of the universe; but as far as the order of physical life, it proceeds according to laws. If one conforms to physical laws, positive results follow. If one breaks physical law, there is not success at that point. If one understands the law of inertia, he is enabled to drive his car with moderate success. If I do not understand something of the laws of inertia, I shall run off the first curve that I come to. Those things are axiomatic in life. We have seen also that there is moral law in the universe; that God has projected this world according to moral laws as well as physical ones — all being part and parcel of that which we call law.

Our Shorter Catechism has a word about the Ten Commandments. It says, Where is the moral law summarized? Where can you find a brief summary of moral law? And the answer is, The moral law is summarily comprehended in the Ten Commandments. These ten words of Moses form a skeleton, as it were, upon which we build moral fabric; they also form a signpost for the road of life. They are a norm or a standard of living.

These are not wholly original with Moses. Such laws were known in part in Babylon. They grew out of the experience of the race with God. Might we put it this way? These truths are not arbitrary ones. They were not given ex cathedra from God, without any purpose or sequence back of them. They are the expression of the laws of life, put in a manner that men can understand and follow. For instance, it is not wrong to kill a man because the Ten Commandments say it is wrong. The Ten Commandments say it is wrong because there can be no order and stability in life when men kill one another. That Commandment is the expression of a basic law of God in the world and it gives voice to it so that men can understand it readily.

Now the Commandments are familiar to all of you. Let me remind you just in passing that they deal with attitudes toward God, attitudes toward our fellow men. The theme of this whole book is "holiness unto the Lord"; that is, that we recognize the might and the majesty and power of God; that we have awe and reverence in His presence; that we know that there are things in life that are not to be handled carnally; that we are to be reverent. The same thing is true when Jesus taught us to pray, the first thing He said, "When thou prayest, say Our Father, which art in heaven, hallowed be Thy Name." Reverence precedes prayer. Reverence is back of the moral law. There is only one God. You are not to have Him duplicated in forms and ceremonies. You are to respect His name, not blaspheme. You are to remember Him by public worship, setting aside one day especially for that worship. God's unity, God's form, His name, and His worship, in the first part.

But the second part deals with our relationship toward our fellow men. We are to respect his material substance, we are to respect his family life, his life itself. We are not to defame him by gossip or slander. We are not to covet through avarice that which he has. A man's name and family and life and reputation and his possessions — these are to be respected, if there is to be order in the world.

One does not have to have much of an imagination to picture the kind of society there would be if there were no laws to govern our actions: if we could pillage and murder and profane whenever we cared to. That is the definition of anarchy, if you desire one.

The transitional commandment, of course, between God and neighbors, is the attitude in the family, to honor thy father and thy mother. Family love and reverence.

You see then that the Westminster Fathers were not afield when they claimed that the moral law of the universe is summarized in the Ten Commandments. The book of Leviticus has many comments on the activities of men toward one another and toward God, summarized here in Moses' statement, that thou shalt love thy neighbor as thyself. That came to me some years ago almost as a discovery. I studied Leviticus very carefully when I was in college. I studied it in part in the original Hebrew. No one ever emphasized to me that particular verse, Thou shalt love thy neighbor as thyself. It seems in a way to be alien to this book, for the law had not recognized at this point Christ's attitude, for Christ had not come. Men had not developed quite far enough along the line of living and the ladder of love to understand this.

For instance let me remind you of this, that in this very book,

Moses said if a man knocks out your eye knock out his; if he knocks out a tooth, knock out one of his. An eye for an eye and a tooth for a tooth. Whatever a man does to you, it is perfectly all right to retaliate in substance and kind. That was the commonly accepted view, but Moses goes beyond it in saying, "Thou shalt love thy neighbor as thyself," meaning, of course, any fellow Hebrew; anyone within the congregation of the Tribes; you must love him as you love yourself.

On this Christmas pre-Sunday, let us examine the Christian attitude. A man came to Jesus one day and he said, "Master, what must I do to gain eternal life?" Christ said, All right; what do you read in the law of Moses? The man replied, I read in the book of Deuteronomy, 'Thou shalt love the Lord thy God with all thy heart, mind, soul, strength, and body,' and I read in the book of Leviticus that 'thou shalt love thy neighbor as thyself.' "Thou shalt love the Lord thy God, and thy neighbor as thyself." Jesus replied, "Thou art right. This do, and thou shalt live."

It would be well to keep that in mind always. Eternal life is not built on the acceptance of the creed, fine expression as that is. It is not based on one's attitude toward the Bible, wonderful inspiration that it is. It does not consist of belonging to this church or that, satisfactory as they are. What Jesus Christ said without equivocation, that if man would have eternal life, he must love God and his neighbor as himself.

That's enough Christmas message for me, for I recognize — as I am certain that you do, that if everything else were destroyed, that would be challenge enough. And Jesus exemplified what He meant by his neighbor when He used the Samaritan as an illustration. If you want to know how difficult Christianity is, just say to yourself that if I am going to have eternal life, I must love God and Stalin as myself. I must love God, and Hitler as myself. I am to love God, and the worst outcast in Lexington as myself. Is that hard? People will rush to you at once and say it's impossible. Christianity is a difficult thing. May I say reverently, My God, how difficult it is! No wonder we do not practice it fully.

It is not some milk-and-water religion. It is something that cuts absolutely across human nature. You will say, That's contrary to human nature, and I reply at once, It is contrary to human nature. Jesus Christ cuts across our human nature and He says, You have to about-face. You must learn to respect everyone. You must learn to realize that everyone is a child of God.

I do not like Stalin, I do not admire Stalin, I do not agree with Stalin, I will oppose Stalin, I will do all of those things; but at the same time I must remember that Stalin is a child of God, and though I feel that he is a very harmful influence, the most harmful in the world, think how God Almighty grieves over the evil going out from that man and his followers. If the heart of God suffers because of those men, then cannot I remember that they are children of God. Oppose them, yes. When you say you love a person as a Christian, it does not mean that you like them necessarily. It is pretty hard to like some people. At least I know a few that it is pretty hard to like, but it is a different matter from loving them in a Christian way. You might think on the difference between affection and loving them as far as Christianity is concerned.

So much for the Law. The second place, the worship and the tabernacle is described in all the minutiae, both in Exodus and Leviticus. We will not dwell there. We do not worship in a tabernacle, nor do we worship in a temple; but it is well historically to remember the development of worship, and we come to the matter of the sacrifices. They taught this: that when a man breaks the Ten Commandments at any point, he is to confess his sins before the priests there in the Temple and he is to make restitution. He is to offer a sacrifice. And this book deals with sacrifices in the Temple.

Now I must admit that when I read it again this past week, it seemed very strange to me. We are a long way from heave offerings and burnt offerings and blood offerings. We couldn't possibly do it. It is back in a kindergarten stage as it were, of the development of religion. They wanted to have exercises that they could see and feel and participate in. So if I sinned, there was a kind of graduating scale, and for some sins I offered a certain kind of sacrifice, and for my heinous ones, a different kind; and they brought all manner both of vegetables and meal and of animals; but the greatest sacrifice was the sacrifice of an animal—when the blood flowed, the blood meant life. They gave life for sin.

That, I say, seemed to be essential at that stage of their development. But as their religion grew, they recognized that it was impractical, or rather insufficient. David in writing his great hymn of contrition said, "A broken and a contrite heart thou wilt not despise." That is what is needed when men sin—a broken and a contrite heart.

Then later on in the prophets we read: Said God, "I despise your burnt offerings. I despise your blood offerings. What doth the Lord require of thee?" Not rivers of oil and rivers of blood, but "What doth the Lord require of thee but to do justly, love mercy, and walk humbly with thy God." While Leviticus is a very beautiful portrayal of a certain stage of their development, it ended at a definite period.

When did it end? It ended on the first Christmas Day. Jesus Christ came into the world to let men see what God is like, to give us an example to follow, and to save us from our sins. You who studied with me this fall the book of Hebrews will remember this. There the writer, sending out a message to the men and women who had been trained in the Levitical way—in all the order of priests and sacrifices, and the High Priest entering in offering up a sacrifice of blood, said that Jesus Christ had come, that He made the sacrifice once and for all. Christ was once offered up for the sins of many. When Jesus Christ hung upon the Cross, when He made this protest against sin, when sin killed Him, when we identify ourselves with Him in our attitude toward sin, when we die unto sin with Him, He has once for all offered up the sacrifice.

So when you read the book of Leviticus, you see the ceremony and the form and that which was essential for them to recognize, and then you turn over to Hebrews and you see another form and another symbol, of Jesus Christ on the cross, once and for all offered up as a sacrifice. When did it start? It started on Christmas Day. Everything prior to Christ was built around form and ceremony; everything after Christ was built on faith and belief. The sin that I commit is just as heinous as that for which the High Priest entered into the Holy of Holies, but as I recognize my sin and identify myself with God in Christ in suffering for my sin, He grants me absolution for my sin. And so it is not necessary to do penance in the form of candles burning or of buying prayers, or doing this and that and the other thing in a mechanical way. But it is entering into the holy of holies of my own heart and saying unto God, God forgive me, miserable sinner that I am. And the Babe of Bethlehem who became the High Priest of mankind touches me upon my heart; and there is penitence and there in His divine forgiveness, I find not only pardon for my sin but strength and power to live His way in the world.

There could be no Christianity without Leviticus, but there can no longer be a Leviticus without Christianity. "Thou shalt love thy neighbor as thyself."

A PEAK IN DARIEN

December 31, 1950
Scripture: Deuteronomy 34:1-12

For our New Year meditation, we come to the fifth book in our study of the Bible—the book of Deuteronomy, which means the second law. We find here a recapitulation of that which was given in the third and fourth books of the Old Testament.

I have chosen for the subject of my sermon today those words that close Keats' poem, *On First Looking Into Chapman's Homer*, "a peak in Darien." The reason that those words came into my mind as I was thinking of the new year and of Moses on Mt. Nebo is very apparent. May I read the concluding lines of that short poem:

Then felt I like some watcher of the skies
When a new planet swims within his ken,
Or like stout Cortez, when with eagle eyes
He stared at the Pacific, and all his men
Looked at each other with a wild surmise.
Silent, upon a peak in Darien.

(Of course it was not Cortez, but Balboa, who stood upon a peak in Darien and looked out upon the Pacific, the first of the Spanish conquerors in the New World.)

Men have looked always to the west from peaks in Darien; so it is an old, old story that we read here: "and Moses went up from the plains of Moab unto the mountain of Nebo to the top of Pisgah; and the Lord showed him all the land." There on Nebo's mountain, this side of the Jordan River, the Lord showed him the land from Dan-Gilead in the north to Judah in the south, the Mediterranean Sea nestling some sixty miles to the west. He stood upon a peak in Darien and looked to the west, long before "bold Cortez" and his men crossed the Isthmus of Panama and looked into the western sea.

Always men stand upon a Nebo or Darien. We look to the west, and we glance back to the east. On New Year's Eve and New Year's Day, because we have divided time so that we may live more effectively, we look back over the year and the years that have gone, and we endeavor as did Moses and Cortez to look forward into the future, ascertaining if possible that which lies ahead. So today as we come to the New Year season, and as we finish the Pentateuch, we stand with Moses on Nebo and look out over the land that is ahead.

The very interesting thing about that story is also that Moses knew that he could not enter into the land. He had lived and worked and pled, he had served his God and his people; but he had struggled for eighty years for that moment, to bring the children of Israel into the Promised Land. Now he stood looking into the Promised Land, but he knew that it was not for him to go over the river. His life ceased at that point.

So it is often, in fact always, no one ever enters a Promised Land in this world. We work, we strive, we arrive at the edge of the Promised Land. We never enter, because the Promised Land always is just ahead. If one should finally achieve all of his ideals, and all of his aims, he would die. There would be nothing left. Goethe recognized that, you know, in Faust; for the compact with the devil was that as soon as Faust was completely satisfied and said, "Stay, thou art fair," then the devil would take him. Whenever anyone ceases to be driven by a divine discontent, then his life is over. "My purpose holds," said old Ulysses, "my purpose holds to sail beyond the sunset and the baths of all the western stars until I die." My purpose holds to sail — where? Always to the west; on and on until I die.

The Lord took Moses on Nebo's mountain and showed him the Promised Land. Thus ends the book of Deuteronomy. May we glance back very briefly at what that book holds; for it is a resume of the last three books.

There are five things that I would remind you of; first, that it has a summary of the moral laws that Moses gave. We have seen how these laws were necessary for life; necessary then and today, that men have a standard and a code by which they go. Then he had the liturgical worship, wherein men expressed themselves, where they communed with God and where they made sacrifices unto God. No longer are such sacrifices needed, the sacrifices of God being a broken and a contrite heart. He does not want blood-offerings, but He wants our love, our humility, our devotion. So this book deals much with worship.

There has been in the country recently much thought on worship. I daresay all over the United States today people will worship in church or in privacy that have not done so for a long time. We realize of course the need of God. Man's plans go awry. The world falls about our ears in spite of ourselves. To whom shall I go except God? Do not leave worship out of your lives. Nothing else suffices. One may have all kinds of gifts and discipline, but unless there is a time set apart for communion with God, we are incomplete. This book stresses the ceremony of worship, beauty of worship; and as we recognize most of these books have an overtone far beyond the page itself, then we know that what Moses taught still holds true for us — that we should worship God in the beauty of holiness.

Also he stressed education, putting these precepts upon their foreheads even, upon the garments that they wore, over their houses, teach them in the homes: "Hear, O Israel, the Lord thy God is one God and Him only shalt thou serve." So the book stresses education.

We find that Deuteronomy also has much to say about their government, their form of government within the tribes and the families and the nation. This nation was a theocracy, ruled from above; but in a theocracy, even where God is the ruler, man needs, must have rules and regulations to follow. Sometimes we find laws irksome, and justly so in some instances of course; but we should remember always that our society is built on the Jewish-Christian conception of the individual, and our city government and state government and national Constitution all have their release not only in the petition of rights and the Bill of Rights and Magna Carta; but far, far beyond that into Deuteronomy and the sermon on the Mount. We have had ingrained in us the life and the worth of the individual and the fact that we are God's children. So when we go back to Deuteronomy and read these old laws, many of them of course no longer needed, we find that our present system of laws is based on their fundamental conception of the human being and of God.

There is another kind of law in these books, and we have a resume in Deuteronomy; the sanitary laws. Some of these sanitary laws seem rather primitive to us, but it was a primitive society. Now we go far beyond it in the knowledge of the body and of the need of society in building health laws. But back in Deuteronomy they had very definite sanitary laws. Why? Well, there is no separation of the body and spirit. One does not say, I live a spiritual life and I live a carnal life—I live with the body and I live with the mind. We want a sound mind in a sound body. Our bodies are temples of the living God; so part of our religion is the proper care of our bodies. Mind over matter, matter over mind, but the spirit over all. So part of one's religion is the proper attitude toward his body, and also to health in society.

It was not for naught that John Calvin, four hundred years

ago in the city of Geneva, made plans and regulations that now the superintendent of health in a community makes. He knew that religion and proper drains go together. There is no such thing as separating the body and the spirit, and religion from health. So there are sanitary laws in the book of Deuteronomy.

There you are: spirit, worship, education, law, and sanitation, all summarized for the Jews in Deuteronomy, with the overtones coming down to us. But that seems a long time ago. What does it mean for us today?

If I am going to stand with Moses on Mt. Nebo and look across Jordan to the Mediterranean, I should like to know what his policies were, what traits of character were his that helped him. What do I need today as I stand at the end of the first half-century of the twentieth century, as I anticipate a new year? I look back, and I look forward. What did Moses have? What can I have to follow him?

When I look back, what do I see? Perhaps the most trying half century in the memory of man — or one of the most. Two world wars, for one thing; and a world-wide depression for another. All of my adult life has been lived in wars and rumors of wars, and the results of war; and you who are my age have had the same experience. What is behind us, and what is in front of us?

These are the characteristics that Moses had that I believe are helpful to me. The first was humility. Moses was meek, says the Bible, above all the people in the earth. He had humility. So as I look back and look forward, if there is going to be satisfaction in my life, I must have humility. That is a very easy thing to say, but very difficult to practice. We are arrogant over so many things. Some are arrogant over their intellectual equipment, and others are arrogant over their family history, while others take pride in their material resources. So many people, almost all people at one time or another, say, I thank God that I am not as this poor publican, either in the realm of intellect of material resources or opportunities or society or what-have-you; we say, I thank God that I am not

193

as this poor publican. I thank God that I am not as these Koreans and Japanese and Germans and so on, that I am a favored, chosen people. The first quality of Moses — a man of whom they said no prophet had arisen in Israel such as he — was humility.

My friends, I am talking to myself and then to you. Let me question myself upon the eve of this new year, whether I have an humble heart and spirit, or whether there is pride and arrogance separating me from God and my proper place in life.

The second thing that he had was faith — not only was he humble, but he had faith. He dared to reach out into the unseen and take hold upon the promises of God, the invincible surmise of life — faith. Now, if I face this new year without faith, I am defeated already. There is no need for me to even think of satisfaction in the coming days if I have no faith. It is the bedrock of life.

The great saying in the Old Testament, you know was that of Job: "Though He slay me, yet will I trust Him." My friends, do you believe in the eternal purposes of God? Do you believe, with Paul, that "all things work together for good to those that love God?" Do you believe that God works in and through history, in and through you and me for His end? Do you believe that truth always conquers in the end? That with God one man is a majority? Do we have that faith? Are we willing to say in spite of everything, We believe that the world marches to fulfill the purposes of God? Slowly, yes. I myself may be lost in the process. I and my loved ones may be blotted out in a physical way in the process. We may go through great suffering, great deprivations; but always if we will have faith, we know that life goes on in the economy of God.

God is not asleep. God has not gone on a journey, but through the natural processes of life, His purpose holds and goes on. Moses knew that. Moses had dreamed of the Promised Land, but he couldn't go in. But he didn't stop. He knew that his end was coming, but the children of Israel were to go on. God said, There it is: look at it, Moses — the land of milk and honey. Look at the blue waters of the Mediterranean miles away, opening into a new world.

There it is, Moses—that is what you have been striving for. You will not get in it physically, but there it is. And Moses had believed in God throughout all the years, and he moved on because he was a man of faith.

Which leads to the third characteristic, which is a part of faith. He was a man of steadfastness. You recall at the end of the life of our Lord Jesus, it was said of Him that He steadfastly set His face to go to Jerusalem. Well, that was Moses. He had steadfastly set his face. He put his teeth into that thing; he took hold with it with his hands and turned not back from his efforts. He stayed with it. Come what may this year, am I willing to stay with it, with the purposes of God? Am I going to be a man of humble heart and spirit and faith in the Eternal and with steadfastness to follow the path, to stay with it?

I am no Moses, nor are you. We are people of varying talents, but all of us can meet on that level of humility, and faith, and steadfastness during the coming year. There I would stop except for one incident that occurs much later in the Bible. I do not know, my friends, I cannot speak with certainty—it seems to me, however, that there is a glorious symbolism in the postlude to this story. It certainly agrees with my philosophy, or my philosophy agrees with it, I hasten to say. You cannot speak with absolute certainty.

The scene changes. Centuries after, Jesus of Nazareth came into the world—the Son of God to save His people, to save you and me. In the latter part of His life, He was going down to Jerusalem to face His capture and crucifixion; and this knowledge drove Him hard. He went up one night on another mount, taking three of His friends with Him—Peter, James, and John. There as they slept, these three young men, they were awakened by a light and they saw a vision—a vision of Jesus with two men. The two men were Elijah—My lord Elijah, the Jews called him, the great prophet in the book of Kings—and Moses. Elijah and Moses talking to Jesus. Moses had now entered the Promised Land.

What does Luke say? This very significant thing—that they

195

were there, Moses and Elijah, to prepare Jesus for His coming death in Jerusalem. What a consummation of a life. He didn't go in with the tribes, but he came in later to prepare our Lord for His death. Nothing could have equaled that climax.

I will come to the end some day, and no one knows when. Many who worshiped here last January 1 no longer worship in the flesh. My brethren, I on Sunday mornings see not only a visible congregation but an invisible congregation that would be larger than this, of members who have died in my own ministry here. And so somebody, some of us, will not be here in the flesh the next few years. But what do we believe? Why, when we stand and look on with that wild surmise of Cortez' men and of Moses looking into the Promised Land—what happens? There comes a time when I shuffle off this mortal flesh and go into the Beyond. But do I stop? Not at all. For if God used Moses to comfort Jesus Christ, God will use you and me throughout all the years that are ahead. Those who worshiped with us in years gone by have not stopped worshiping nor have they stopped living and being creative in God's Kingdom; nor will you. Seventy years, eighty years, ninety years— just a breath in God's sight.

God will use me in the Promised Land. While Moses hated to go, strong, vigorous, great leader; he did. But that was not the end of Moses. He returned to strengthen our Lord.

Today, as I stand upon a peak in Darien, silently looking out over the western sea, I know that with God all things are well; and that my loved ones and you and I will live out His consummation throughout all the ages.

AN AGE OLD QUESTION

March 11, 1951
Scripture: Job 42:1-9

In our study of the books of the Bible we come today to Job, and for a text I am taking words from the seventh verse of this 42nd chapter: "The Lord said to Eliphaz the Temanite, My wrath is kindled against thee and against thy two friends: for ye have not spoken of me the thing that is right, as my servant Job hath." Those words, "for ye have not spoken of me the thing that is right, as my servant Job hath."

The book of Job is perhaps the greatest literary masterpiece in all the Bible. We lose sight of that fact in reading the King James version, for it is not placed in the metrical form in which it was written. I rather think that critics, apart from Biblical students, would place it in the forefront of poems in all languages of all times. It is a very great book.

We do not know when it was written; probably rather late in the history of the Jews, some time in the fifth century before Christ. Nor do we know the name of the author. Nowhere is it given or implied. However, we see that he was a great genius, a poet of the first rank, a man who had wide knowledge, one of profound thought. In fact, as we read this book we discover that Job is one of the great rebels of all time; one of the iconoclasts, as it were, in history; who broke with the tradition of his people, and once

197

and for all sounded a note that men might follow.

This author was an original thinker, having keen insight into human life. Now I daresay you do not read the book of Job very often. It has overtones that are sad. A name has been given to his friends, "Job's comforters," which gives you the idea that it is pessimistic and discouraging, depressing. Yet for pure imagery in speech and sheer beauty, there are passages that cannot be excelled. Might I read you just one very short one, illustrating the beauty of the poetry. I have here in my hand a copy of the book of Job, illustrated in a very striking manner, the format is good and it is arranged in its poetical form. Let me read you just a few lines from one of Job's speeches:

> But where shall wisdom be found?
> Where is the place of understanding?
> Man knoweth not the price thereof,
> Neither is it found in the land of the living.
> The depth sayeth, It is not in me;
> And the sea sayeth, It is not with me.
> It cannot be gotten for gold,
> Neither shall silver be weighed for the price thereof.
> It cannot be valued with the gold of Ophir,
> With the precious onyx or the sapphire.
> The gold and crystal cannot equal it,
> And the exchange of it shall not be for jewels or fine gold.
> No mention shall be made of coral or of pearls,
> For the price of wisdom is above rubies.
> The topaz of Ethiopia shall not equal it,
> Neither shall it be valued with pure gold.
> Whence then cometh wisdom,
> And where is the place of understanding,
> Seeing it is hid from the eyes of all living
> And kept close from the fowls of the air?
> Destruction and death say, We have heard the fame thereof with our ears,

God understandeth the way thereof.
And He knoweth the place thereof.
For He looketh to the ends of the earth
And seeth under the whole heaven,
To make the wake for the winds,
And He weigheth the waters by measure.
When He made a decree for the rain
And a way for the lightning of the thunder,
Then did He see it and declare it;
He prepared it, yea, and searched it out,
And unto man He said,
Behold, the fear of the Lord, that is wisdom,
And to depart from evil is understanding.

"The price of wisdom is above rubies," and "the fear of the Lord, that is wisdom," "and to depart from evil is understanding." That very brief quotation, I am certain, will give you some evidence and indication of the beauty of the book.

Now I said that this book is the answer to an age old question, or rather it is an attempt at an answer to that question. When you finish the book, you realize that the question has not been answered completely, for after all it cannot be answered in fullness, though the way is indicated. That question is this: Why do innocent people suffer? Why is there sorrow and affliction in the world?

You realize that there are two basic questions in life. Neither of these questions has been answered completely. The first is, Why is there evil in the world? Why is there sin in the human race? The Bible grapples with the question of sin from first to last. That is the whole theme of the Bible; endeavoring to find the way of delivery from evil. But it never answers the question why God allowed sin in the world except in the story of the Garden of Eden, we know it came from the right of free choice, which is perhaps the best answer.

The other question is, Why do people who are good meet

199

with misfortune? Why do innocent people suffer? The Bible teaches that a man is punished for his sins; that ofttimes to the third and fourth generation children pay for the shortcomings of their parents and their forebears. We see evidences of that. And it is just that if I commit a wrong, I pay for it — at least in part, though through God in Christ we are enabled to find forgiveness and sanctification and adoption, as we have studied in days gone by. But why do innocent people suffer? Why does sorrow reach out and touch a man?

That question is just as old as the human race. It is just as present as the minute that I am standing in this pulpit. In the order of the books we came to Job today. I did not artificially choose this; it is just in the sequence we follow. Friday night I went home from a social engagement and there was a phone call saying, Will you please come to a certain home. This is what the message was about. (Might I preface it by saying this, any Sunday morning if you stand in the halls of Sunday School you see lovely children passing, boys and girls from two years old and up; it is a very delightful and stimulating experience to stand there in the halls.) There was a little girl among many who has come for years. She had reached the age of 8, and the phone message was that this little girl eight years old had died Friday afternoon.

A beautiful child she was physically, and a beautiful child in spirit. Really an angelic kind of child. Her mother said to me that perhaps she had been so good and of such angelic nature that it wasn't meant for her to stay in this earth. I went into that home Friday night. The sermon had been completed practically, and here was a present question. Why is a little girl eight years old taken? And why do the parents and grandparents have that sorrow to confront them? You take that and multiply thousands and millions of times all over the world. As someone suggested this morning, Why are thousands of children in Korea, who had nothing to do with the world situation, bombed out?

Of course we know that evil in men brought that on, but

the innocent suffer. So this week any one of us may have the question confronting us: Why did this happen to me? Why do I suffer? Why is it placed in my lap, even as Job had it? Do not think you will escape. You are always open to the adversary. There is not one single person here who may not somewhere along the line this week be confronted with sudden sorrow and with pain, even as this family of which I spoke.

So the man who wrote this book endeavored to answer that question. You see at once that if you could find the answer to that, it would be a great relief. It would be a marvelous thing if we had hold of a truth or truths that would steady us.

Briefly this is the story. It is cast in the form of a dramatic poem. It starts in heaven where God is (the first two chapters, by the way, are in prose, very beautiful prose), before Whom the sons of men. God seeing Satan inquires, Where have you been? The reply is, I have been going to and fro about the Earth. God questioned him, Have you considered my servant Job, that he is a righteous and upright man? Yes, said Satan, I have seen Job; but let me tell you this, if he were touched by adversity he would not be righteous. So God says, All right, you may afflict him. Then Satan afflicts Job. His children lose their possessions and he loses his possessions, his children were killed, and calamity after calamity piled on him. But still he did not curse God.

When Satan returned the second time, God asked again, Do you consider my servant Job? Yes, said he, but let me touch his health, God agreed, anywhere except his life. And so he touched him with that skin disease called boils, evidently in a very malignant, painful form. Job had lost his possessions and his family and now his health. His wife said to him, Why do you not curse God and die? His reply was, Thou speakest as one of the foolish women.

Then the writing changes into poetic form. Here in the preface we are behind the scenes, understanding the mechanism of it. There is a contest, Job is made a testing point between God and the adversary; and we will find how Job meets this. Job's friends come

201

from afar, Eliphaz, Bildad, Zophar. When they first arrived, they had a very beautiful technique. It says they sat down and stayed a week, and for a week they did not open their mouth. They were quiet, sympathetic and understanding.

Then the conversation commences; and as you read the book you will find that there are three rounds of conversation: Job, then Eliphaz. Job, Bildad, Job, Zophar. Round one: then they have round two, the same way; and then round three. After Zophar finishes his final short speech, Job has a long speech. Then a young man sitting by named Elihu breaks in, and Elihu rather summarizes what Eliphaz, Bildad and Zophar have said. After that, God speaks to Job out of the whirlwind. When Job hears God, he said, I have heard of Thee but now I see Thee and I repent in dust and ashes. A postlude is tacked on in prose, which is very unfortunate I think. This postlude was put on because of the dramatic form, but it is not true to life. Everything was restored to Job—his health and his possessions and his family. That's not the way it works usually in life. We lose these things and they're gone with the wind forever.

So there is the setting. Great dramatic poem, a great epic poem, if you will. If you will get some edition of the Bible that has the poetic form, you can follow it better. Mark off these divisions, the speeches and the rounds, and it stands out more clearly. Now basically this is what happened in these speeches. The friends held to a view that was common among men, and strangely enough it is still held by some people. That view was this: that the righteous prosper and the evil suffer. Therefore, if a person meets with adversity it is a sign that he has sinned. The righteous prosper; the evil suffer; if you have met with adversity, it is a sign that you have sinned. Now I say that fallacy still persists in life.

Two illustrations there would be enough. After President Coolidge retired from the White House, he wrote his autobiography. Somewhere in it he told of the death of one of his sons. You remember the boy was playing tennis on the White House court and rubbed his heel which became infected, and he died. President Coolidge said this: The death of the boy was the price that God exacted of me for the presidency. It is the same old argument of Eliphaz. God didn't take that boy because Coolidge was president.

Years ago I was in a Presbyterian minister's home up in northeast West Virginia, teaching in a conference. In the home there had been two sons, and one of the boys a few years before had been drowned over in Lexington, Virginia. He was a student in Washington and Lee. The mother in talking about it said to my companion and me (we were two Presbyterian preachers), God took my boy to punish me for my sins. We said, Never say that, Mrs. So-and-so. God is the Father of our Lord Jesus Christ and He loves us all. He does not reach out and take our children or anyone to punish us. She replied, You are strange Presbyterian ministers. We did not argue the point, but I felt like telling her, You are a disciple of Eliphaz, and Bildad, and Zophar.

This reminds me of an aside. Many years ago I was sitting in on a young people's debate, and an older man could not restrain himself. He was like Elihu. He broke in to refute one of the young people and he quoted, An eye for an eye; all that a man hath will he give for his life. Then he sat down. He thought he had refuted the youth. Well then, I could not stand it, so I had to get up and say, Mr. Moderator, I did not mean to speak; but all that I would remind you of is this, that this gentleman was quoting what the devil said in the book of Job. You see, the devil can quote Scripture with effect or authority, said Shakespeare.

In the first round these three men held out this general view. But Job maintains his innocency, that he had not sinned, that he was not responsible for this. On the second round the friends begin to warm up a little to it, and they imply that after all, Job, you have had some hidden sin that hasn't come out, and God is punishing you for that which we know not of. But Job still maintained his innocency.

Have you ever heard comments like this? There'll be some

Godly man or woman whose boy or girl has done something disreputable or discrediting. People will say, Well, you know it's rather strange. Probably Mr. So-and-so, whose son has discredited him, was doing some things that we do not know about. That old idea that this retribution will get you.

Now Job maintained his innocency. But when he really begins to warm up, this is what he says. He shakes his fist at God. I am reminded of the story of St. Theresa, the Spanish saint that had taken a tour through Spain. Sometimes I have felt the same way on these Sundays we have had. She, coming back from a long trip was crossing the river on a barge. The heavens opened and wet her to the skin. Already she had suffered much with the journey. St. Theresa stood in the bow and shook her fist at the heaven and said, "No wonder men hate You for the way You do." People curse God at times. I haven't cursed God, but I've thought that the Lord didn't have much interest in the weather the last three months on Sundays. (Might I just put that in as an aside.)

Here Job said, You have beset me behind and before; you have fenced me in, and I am innocent. He hurls his defiance at God, that No, I have not sinned. I am righteous, I do not deserve this. But he goes on the next step in maintaining his integrity, taking this leap of faith—one of the great leaps of faith in the Bible and all mankind. He said to God, these have all happened to me, but though You slay me, yet will I trust You.

When you can say that, you've gone a long way. "Though He slay me, yet will I trust Him." He goes further. He maintains his innocency, he protests to God that he is righteous, he resents the interference of God, but he says, Though He slay me, yet will I trust Him. Then beyond that, listen: "I know that my Redeemer liveth. I know that my Redeemer liveth, and though worms shall consume this flesh, yet I shall stand before Thee in the last day." A general rendering of that passage, that he would be vindicated after death. That is where Job comes, but when he says these things, what do the friends do? They really take him apart in the last round.

They said, Job, you old scoundrel, you have robbed widows and defrauded children. You have been evil; and they just piled epithet upon epithet, because he stood out against their theory. You see, he was one of the greatest rebels; that this thing is not true. Mark you, at the end what did God say? I took it for my text. "My wrath is kindled against thee," that is Eliphaz and his friends, "and against thy two friends: for ye have not spoken of me the thing that is right, as my servant Job hath." Job withstood God, but he withstood this fallacy, that only evil people suffer.

Then at the end God speaks to him out of the whirlwind. Go home and read that. Where were you at the creation of the world, when the morning stars sang together — and he talks of the heaven and the sea and the earth and the animals on it. He goes on and on about the glory and the magnificence of God. The conclusion is this (and I leave it with you; it is inconclusive, but it is this): that our finite minds cannot grasp God. God did not explain to Job why these things happened. He left it in the lap of Job realizing that there is an infinite Mind over against our finite minds. There are problems in the world we can never quite understand in this life. But the faith that a man holds in God eventually will work it out.

I could not stop there. There is another word. Here is the final word, that when Jesus Christ came, God Himself suffered. God could not escape pain, any more than Job or any more than you; for in Christ God suffered, and in us God suffers. So the heart of God is touched today because Julie Shields died at eight, and the heart of God sorrows because thousands of Korean children die, and the heart of God grieves for all our pains; for He is touched with the spirit of our infirmities. So on the cross in the suffering of Christ, God is linked up with the whole human race in suffering; and the highest plane is not doing the will of God or experiencing the resurrection, high as they are. It is that we are bound with Him and with one another in a fellowship of suffering.

Job is so profound that one can only touch the edges of it; but suffering is so universal that only God knows the final answer.

REBUILDING RUINED CITIES

July 8, 1951
Scripture: Amos 9:9-15

There are names of certain towns in the world that are famous because of people that have come from them; for when you consider the size of the community and its location, you would know that there would be no fame connected with them. I think of such a place as Hodgenville, Kentucky, which is not great among the cities of our commonwealth, yet in a way is the most famous of all of them because of Abraham Lincoln. In northeastern France the village of Domremy will always be known because Jean d'Arc came from there. On the banks of the Potomac there is not even a settlement now at Wakefield where George Washington grew up. And so it goes throughout the world. Little towns and hamlets are written large on the pages of history because of those that went therefrom.

So it is with a hamlet in Judea called Tekoa; for from Tekoa which was on the highlands above the valley of the Dead Sea, not so many miles from Jerusalem, there started out one day a herdsman and a dresser of vineyards named Amos, who went north some 50 miles to a well known place called Bethel and there began to preach. This happened around 750 years before Christ. No one had ever heard of Amos outside of that small community. As long as men live, his message will be repeated. He is one of the most extraordinary characters in all the history of men, for he discovered through the Divine Will certain underlying precepts of life. Not only did he discover them but he proclaimed them to his fellow men and then they were preserved in manuscript form.

I have spoken much of the history of the Jews, how after the division of the kingdom, the northern capital was at Samaria, the southern at Jerusalem. As the northern kingdom went its bloody way, it reached its highest power and wealth under a man named Jeroboam II. In his reign Amos prophesied. The threatening power of Assyria was in another generation to destroy the northern kingdom; but in the lull before that storm they had more wealth and greater ease than at any time in their history. Their production was at its highest rate; their income was greater than ever before. Their ease and their pleasure was more evident to the eye. In the center of worship at Bethel, where they had the golden calf, the ritual had attained an added magnificence. Men felt that here in their place of worship they were reaching out to God, and one day this wild prophet from the south appeared.

I say he was wild. Perhaps he was not. For when the high priest spoke of him, condemning his utterances and endeavoring to banish him from the country, he replied, "No prophet am I, nor am I a prophet's son. I am a herdsman and also a keeper of vineyards. There is within me, though," said he, "this compelling message from God." Amos spoke his piece, and he wrote it, and it has been preserved.

Our time does not permit, nor would I tax your patience on a July Sunday, to outline this book too carefully. But I would mention three things that Amos said; the three main points of his prophecy. When you read the book, you discover at once that a certain inclusive word is left out. Love is not mentioned in Amos. He did not reach the heights of Hosea or Micah or Isaiah or Jeremiah in

207

that respect. He was the forerunner of these men. He antedated them, and in his emphasis on other truths he paved the way for love. What was his message then? Briefly, three things he spoke of, three marks of a degenerate people.

Now we do not consider ourselves a degenerate people, degenerate in the sense that we are disintegrating. Yet always we should take heed. Here in this year when we are 175 years old as a nation, we should examine ourselves for the sins of Israel are still prevalent, and they can be destructive to us as they were to Israel. What were the three marks that he mentioned? Briefly this: the cruel negligence of the rich, the injustice of the rulers, and their false worship. Money, justice, worship: those three approaches to life.

This is what he said to the people of Israel. "Woe to those that are at ease in Zion, who recline upon ivory couches, who have the finest of the lands and the flocks, who drink wine from golden goblets, who devour the poor," marking the various manifestations of wealth in that community, and ending this way: "but they are not grieved for the affliction of Joseph." "Woe to those that are at ease in Zion . . . for they are not grieved for the affliction of Joseph."

The Bible does not condemn money, nor does it condemn wealth. When we listen to Amos speak of those that are at ease in Zion, we must take heed whether we are people of wealth, or moderate circumstances. We are to think in terms of the place of money in our lives. St. Paul said later on, "The love of money is the root of all evil." Notice, he did not say money is the root of all evil, but the love of money is the root of all evil. Now one may be ever so poor and have the love for money that he is harmed, as a man may be ever so rich and have a love for money and suffer ill. If we are at ease in Zion.

Briefly might I remind you of this: that what Amos was speaking of was the indifference of people to their fellow man; their complacency, their desire for ease and comfort, their self-indulgence—all of these things that centered on self and they were not grieved for the affliction of Joseph. In other words, they cared not if other people suffered, as long as they had what they wanted. They took no interest in their fellow man, as long as their wants were supplied. Beware of being at ease in Zion.

Now that was a complicated situation, my friends. It was not new in Amos' time; it is still present with us. I cannot hope to give you the solution here in one morning's meditation on money. We have that constant dualism in our nature between acquisitiveness and generosity. We are trained to acquire possessions, and we are taught to part with possessions. We say to young people, "You must learn how to make a living," and at the same time we say, "you must learn how to give." Take in with one hand and put out with the other, and it's very difficult to balance. Also, it is natural to love possessions—a nice home, furniture, and clothing, for ourselves and our children and our loved ones; to have a competence in life; to live pleasantly and graciously. That is perfectly all right, we say; and it is. But at the same time, said Amos, the danger is that we do not grieve for the affliction of Joseph.

While we are at ease, others suffer. While we live in delightful homes, others are in trouble. While we have more than we can consume, others have not enough. And men have wrestled with that problem all through the years. I used to think in my immaturity that perhaps economics could be made an exact science. So far in my life I have not been able to discover anyone that could make economics an exact science. No one seems to be able to control or anticipate all of the cycles economically. Nor has the state or community or the church been enabled to correct many abuses though all are trying. What I would say to you today from the Bible is, not from the standpoint of the state or the standpoint of the community, for you release yourselves as citizens in that sphere. But I would remind myself as a Christian endeavoring to follow Amos and Jesus Christ, that I am to start with myself and my own understanding—that I am not to be so much at ease in Zion that I shall ever forget the affliction of Joseph.

All you have to do is to ride around the city, any day, any time, and it will keep you from being at ease in Zion. It will make you uncomfortable in Zion. It will cause you to feel more of a responsibility for your fellow man. And then you will begin to seek means to release yourself into these places. Good housing will help some, birth control will help some, other social and scientific means will help some. A man with eight or ten children on a day laborer's wages cannot bring the child up so he can have a fair chance in the community. But apart from these scientific and social acts or approaches, the basic thing is for me to remember that I am not to be at ease in Zion. I am to be mindful of the affliction of Joseph, and in some way release myself into life so that things will be made better.

When I get into that field, I may then begin to contend in political measures, social measures, and scientific ones and differ with my fellows. But I must have the basic drive and understanding that I am not to be at ease in Zion. Do not think that is just if you are wealthy. Not at all. It is for any grade of economic living, to be mindful of the affliction of Joseph.

The second thing that he spoke of was the injustice. Let righteousness prevail. "Ye who turn judgement to wormwood, and leave off righteousness in the earth, for I know your mainfold transgressions and your mighty sins. They afflict the just, they take a bribe, and they turn aside the poor." They take a bribe, they afflict the just, and turn aside the poor. "Seek good and not evil, that ye may live. Hate the evil, and love the good, and establish judgement in the gates."

Then he made a marvelous statement: "But let judgement run down as waters and righteousness as a mighty stream." Perhaps the best-known line: "I will set a plumb-line in the midst of my people Israel." Notice then what he talks about : Let righteousness and justice be as a stream. These people that are not just, who afflict the poor, who take bribes — have you ever heard in America of anybody taking bribes, or perverting justice or oppressing the poor or exalting evil? Well, all you have to do is read the newspaper any day, and you know that these sins are in our midst.

Today they are in our midst. Amos tells those people long ago that God will not countenance such living. And he used that figure, that he would drop a plumb-line. Masons you know use a plumb-line; bricklayers, when they are building a wall, drop that plumb-line. I had an illustration of that the other day. It has been just a year since the congregation voted to save the spire—a great day in our church, I assure you. And so they started to rebuild the spire, and up in the top of the steeple they dropped a line, a plumb-line, so that the steeple would be true. They had engineers off at the side with transepts to measure to see that it was true. I was talking to one of our friends across the street the other day, one of the business men in the business right across the street. He told me he watched the steeple every day, and toward the end when they were getting it into line, one day it would be an inch or two over and then they would pull it back and they finally got it so it was exactly in line. "I will drop a plumb-line" and the steeple is true because it was placed in line with a plumb-line that was there.

That's what God does, said Amos. "I will drop a plumb-line" right into a people. And by that I measure what is right and what is wrong, what is just and what is unjust, what is true and what is false. And to the rulers and the people, do not pervert justice; do not take bribes; do not oppress the poor. In this last week we celebrated our birthday, the 4th of July. That's what the Founding Fathers said, that's what Thomas Jefferson and those other men said—that all men are created equal. Equal where? Well, not intellectually, not economically, not socially. People aren't created equally that way. Some have more sense than others, certainly more opportunities. But our republic is based on the fact that all men are created equal—where? In the sight of Almighty God and in the sight of the law. In the courts of the land, every man has his individual right for life, liberty, and the pursuit of happiness. All of that goes back to Amos. "I will drop a plumb-line," said our Lord.

The last thing he mentioned is this: about their worship. Not only must they not be at ease in Zion, not only must they be just, but they must have real worship. "I hate," said he (notice the word he puts in the mouth of God). "I hate, I despise your feast days, and I will not smell of your solemn assemblies." Fine church, great temple, splendid sacrifices — God said, I'll have none of them. In other words, it takes more than form in worship. You really take a risk when you come to church, do you know it? We put ourselves out on a limb when we go to church (to use a slang expression). Why? Because everybody sees us in church, then begin to have a standard to measure us by. Anyone that is a little sharp in practice or is shady in his business dealings or unkind to his employees or unfair — all through this week, you and I are being measured by the kind of lives we live.

So God said, Not your church service; not your sermon; not your choir; not your music; not all of this beautiful sanctuary and all that you do. It is, He said, very lovely, but that's not the essence of it. That's not the essence of it, you see. Repentance, confession, living out our religion. And so Amos warns us against being at ease in Zion, being unjust in any of our practices, and unrealistic in our religion.

What does it all come to? In that last chapter he says that God is always in the background, God will bring His people through. And one thing caught my eye especially: "He will rebuild the ruined cities."

Have you prayed this week-end? Are you praying now for what will happen in Korea this week? Some day when people stop taking their ease in Zion, and some day when justice and righteousness prevail in the world, some day when there is real unfeigned religious living on the part of people, then ruined cities will be rebuilt and wars will cease. But not until we are redeemed from our complacency and our injustice and our formalism in religion. Pray God that the herdsman from Tekoa will linger in our minds and in our actions.

GREATEST SAYING OF THE OLD TESTAMENT

September 2, 1951
Scripture: Micah 6:1-8

All of us have favorite books of the Bible. As far as I am concerned myself, in the books of prophecy, Micah is my favorite. It has more that stimulates my thought and challenges my attention and my life, within the compass of this short book, of any other in the Old Testament among the prophets. Micah lived in the reign of Hezekiah; he prophesied at the same time that Isaiah was preaching in the capital city. Micah lived in a village called Moresheth in the hill country of the Jews, about half-way from Jerusalem to the coast. There in the hills he could look out over the plains toward the Philistian city of Gath and of Askelon, and going northeast he could be in the capital in a few hours' walk.

Many pilgrims and couriers passed that way. While it was a small community, it was near the center of the nation's capital. Micah, I think, is a fine illustration of the fact that a man does not necessarily occupy a commanding position to have a widespread influence. Isaiah was the preacher in the court; Micah was the preacher in a village. Yet with all the brilliance and beauty of Isaiah, we find no higher truths than in this small book of Micah.

I mention that by way of parenthesis because all too often we are apt to judge a person by the particular position that he occupies. We say, because this man is a minister of a great church he is doing more in the Kingdom than a man in a small one. Or because this man occupies an outstanding position in the state, he is building more constructively than some unknown Christian in a far-away and out of the way place. You recall the story that Wolfe is said to have mentioned on the Plains of Abraham just before his death, that he would rather have written Gray's "Elegy" than to have conquered Montcalm. Gray, the pastor of a small country church, wrote a poem that will live forever. I am quite certain that General Wolfe was right in his evaluation, that it would have been a greater thing to write Gray's "Elegy" than to win the battle of Quebec on the Plains of Abraham.

So here we have this small book, by a country prophet, 700 years before Christ. What a message it has for us today! Within the limits of the time, I would mention three outstanding characteristics. There are other things, but these three suffice.

It is perhaps noteworthy, or coincidental I should say, that on the Sunday before Labor Day we would have the prophecy of Micah; for he has much to say about labor, about working with one's hands, the attitude that people should have in labor. You and I have come to a time that is particularly complicated. We find that capital and labor all too often are arrayed against one another, and that all too often labor (and I say this sympathetically), all too often labor, because it was at the bottom of the pendulum, has overreached itself in the day of its power. That I can say, friendly as I am to the laboring man. But there is to be on the part of all of us Christian relationship within our work.

So notice what Micah says — the first point that I would bring out. He deals with this whole economic attitude; and while he is speaking of land-owners, the same would be true in reverse to those who occupy the land. "Woe to them that devise iniquity, and work evil upon their beds. When the morning is light, they practice it, because it is in the power of their hand. And they covet fields and take them by violence, and houses, and take them away. So they oppress a man and his house, even a man and his heritage." Later on he has much to say about false weights and balances; in other words, Micah probes at the root of the economic order, that there must be justice and fairness on the part of all.

Sometimes we are apt to think the Bible has nothing to say about economics. It is full of it; and while we are careful never to arraign ourselves politically because that is apart from the church, we should never forget the spiritual emphasis — whether we are people of means or poverty, whether we are in one party or another; there are these basic, fundamental truths. And woe to them, said Micah, who in the night-watches devise plans whereby they may defraud their fellow man and as soon as the morning comes put them into execution. So the first point we would remember in Micah is that he has much to say about honesty and fairness in business matters.

The second thing is, that he portrays an ideal world. In his fourth chapter he tells what the ideal world is like. May I refresh your memory on that, for it is one of the great passages in all the Bible. It is interesting to note that it is the same as a part of Second Isaiah. Either Micah borrowed from Isaiah or Isaiah borrowed from Micah, or both quoted some other source. Notice what he says about the ideal world: "But in the last days," that is, in the days when the world has come to its fruition, what Jesus Christ called the Kingdom of God, "But in the last days it shall come to pass that the mountain of the house of the Lord shall be established in the top of the mountains, and it shall be exalted above the hills, and people shall flow unto it. And many nations shall come and say, Come, and let us go up to the mountain of the Lord, unto the house of the God of Jacob. And he will teach us of his ways, and we will walk in his path, for the law shall go forth of Zion, and the word of the Lord from Jerusalem. And he shall judge among many people and rebuke strong nations afar off. And they shall beat their swords into ploughshares, and their spears into pruninghooks. Nation shall not lift up a sword against nation; neither shall they learn war any more. But they shall sit every man under his vine and under his fig tree, and none shall make them afraid, for the mouth of the Lord of hosts hath spoken it."

What a perfectly marvelous conception! And notice there are four characteristics. first, that in the perfect, ideal world, there will be reverence. There will be worship. Men shall say, "Come, and let us go up to the house of the Lord and worship." First, worship and reverence.

The second thing, there shall be no war. Nations shall beat their swords into ploughshares, and their spears into pruninghooks. Tanks shall be turned into tractors, and airplanes into plows, and all of the implements of war into building the agriculture and economy of a nation for peace. There shall be no more war, said Micah.

The third step is that there shall be economic security. "And every man shall sit under his own vine and fig tree." Every man shall own his own little home, if necessary. There shall be enough for all in this world of which Micah spoke and of which Jesus fulfilled. Every man shall sit under his own vine and fig tree.

The fourth, notice: "And none shall make them afraid." There will be confidence. There will be security from fear. How would you like to live in that kind of a world? In which there is worship, and no war, and economic security, and freedom from fear. That's what Micah said is the world that God had in mind.

How does that come? He goes on to tell how it will come. In a most striking verse, the very first time in the Bible that this place is mentioned in connection with the ideal world, so notice what he says there: "But thou, Bethlehem Ephrathah, though thou be little among the thousands of Judah, yet out of thee shall he come forth unto me that is to be ruler of Israel, whose goings forth have been from of old from everlasting." When Jesus came, they remembered that the prophet had said that "thou, Bethlehem Ephrathah, though thou be least among the thousands of Judah, out of thee shall come forth the ruler," the Prince of Peace.

So Micah pictured an ideal world, and then he told us who would bring that ideal world. When Jesus came, He began to talk about the Kingdom of Heaven. He told us all the details of this Kingdom, of this ideal world, of which Micah and Isaiah had sung.

Then the third thing in the book that I would remind you of is this very practical statement that he makes in the end. He said, "I have a controversy with Israel (God had). I brought you out of the land of Egypt, I tended you, but you do not follow me. You have endeavored to know me through a certain form, through the sacrifices of animals, and through pouring out oil and wine. But that's not what I want." They would even go so far as to sacrifice their children. Micah speaks for God in the outstanding verse in all the Old Testament. As George Adam Smith says, there is only one greater verse in the Bible, and that is "Come unto me, all ye that labour and are heavy-laden, and I will give you rest." Notice what he says: "He hath showed thee, O man, what is good."

Might I pause there? I want to know what is good. I like to have a model to follow, for I am apt to become confused in my values. There are so many relative things in the world that we are perplexed. "He hath showed thee, O man, what is good. And what doth the Lord require of thee?" What does He require of the members of First Church and their minister? What is it now? Well notice, three things. He doth "require of thee, but to do justly, and to love mercy, and to walk humbly with thy God." Again I say, a most marvelous saying.

Will you look at it for a moment very briefly as we analyze it? "He hath showed thee what is good" and what does He require of you today and tomorrow, all through this week, all through the coming days, as we endeavor to implement this Kingdom. We are

217

thinking of San Francisco this week, trying to make a step forward in turning these tanks and airplanes into tractors and plows and schools. How are we going about it, you and I? Three ways, said Micah. First, to do justly; to be just.

You notice his attitude there in the social matters about property, and being fair to others. Now we speak of a judicial mind, of being fair and just. I am always interested when I meet a Christian who is fair and just. It is a great attribute. Right after I came to Kentucky I came in contact with a man who had a great reputation as a federal judge. He sat here at the Lexington court: old Judge Cochran, an elder in the Presbyterian Church at Maysville. Judge Cochran was a stormy kind of a man at times; he was certainly forthright. But he was just, he was fair, and when a man went in Judge Cochran's court, either as a lawyer to plead or when he was there as a plaintiff, he knew that there would be absolute fairness and justice. "What doth the Lord require of thee?" Why, to be just and fair and honest. The tradition that Judge Cochran set up has been carried on by his successors, Judge Ford and Judge Swinford, and carried on by many men. And we see evidences of it everywhere, so refreshing.

But in our own lives, we who are not judges should have a judicial mind and be fair and just to our fellow man. "And what doth the Lord require of thee but to do justly."

But in the second requirement, he goes beyond that: "and to love mercy." To love mercy. Mercy, you see, exceeds justice. If the time permitted and it were necessary, I would refresh your minds with those famous words of Shakespeare. "The quality of mercy is not strain'd. It droppeth as the gentle rain from heaven upon the place beneath," and so on. Mercy seasons justice, and is greatest in the mighty. Mercy is an attribute of God. So not only must we be just, but we must be merciful. Dr. Moffat translates that line, "you must be kind." Remember, Paul said, "Be ye kind, one to another, in honor preferring one another." Be ye kind one to another.

218

Every once in a while a statement is made to me, which begins to work in my mind, and I observe life as it comes in contact with it so that it comes out even stronger than it went in. A few years ago someone said to me, The outstanding Christian characteristic is kindness. Kindness is the outstanding Christian characteristic. I replied, "That's a lovely thought." For three years now I have been thinking of that, and I have come to the conclusion that they were dead right, that they were absolutely right: plain, everyday unadulterated kindness is the greatest of all the Christian characteristics. "Be ye kind one to another, in honor preferring one another."

Think of the people that need it. The people that work in the kitchen or on your farm, in your store, in your office, in your schoolroom, in your own home, everywhere people need kindness. You do not have to make any parade of it, but just ordinary kindness. And today on your way home and before tonight or tomorrow, you may by some kind deed touch a person that will lighten the day and the week.

But it goes beyond that. Not only to do justly and to love mercy, but to walk humbly with thy God. To have humility. While kindness may be the outstanding characteristic of a Christian, humility expresses more of maturity in Christian living than anything else. It takes maturity to have humility. One needs to be "rolled around" in life, to use that expression. You have to be disappointed; you have to be defeated; you have to be frustrated. A great many things happen to you, drive you to your knees, to make you realize that you are not the lord of creation; that in your own strength you cannot avail. As a man grows older, he should grow more humble. He should have more humility. He must realize that he hasn't all of the answers; nor is he the pattern of perfection.

We were speaking in a class this morning. A minister, you see, is not a person to tell you how to do. It's not my business to tell you how to live. Not at all. It is my business to share with you the great truths of the Bible and of the world, and together seek the way of life. And if I ever once ventured to tell you what to do, it would be a mark of spiritual pride; for after all, who am I to tell you what to do? That is God's prerogative.

Humble thyself; walk with thy God. There is another translation there, and Dr. Moffat gives it: "To walk in quiet fellowship with God." May I close with this very short story. About ten days ago I ran into a friend of mine down the street and I stopped and chatted with him a minute or two. He had written me a letter that was forwarded, and I had replied from Washington. He is not a member of our church, and I was thanking him again for the letter and he told me he had gotten my reply. This man had had a very serious operation in another city.

When I inquired, "How's your strength coming?" he replied, "It's coming steadily but slowly. I haven't my full strength yet." Then he made this comment: "When I was in the hospital, a man came to see me—a lay-worker in the church. And he said, 'Remember this: you've been in the best hospital that you'll find anywhere for this problem. You've had all the medical attention that a hospital could give you. You've had the finest surgeon for this particular malady. You've had everything that could be done. Now,' said he, 'you have to rely on a Higher Power outside yourself. You've got to have faith. In other words, you have to walk in quiet fellowship with your God.'"

It was a rainy morning and just then his automobile drove up and he said, "Can I give you a lift?" and I said, "No, my car is around the corner." As he stepped across the pavement, he turned and waved, saying, "You know, I believe there's something in that." And I said, "You're absolutely right. There's something in that." Hospital, yes. Surgeon, yes. All that you can do—but over and above that, this power of God; this faith.

You have problems; all of us have them. We do everything we can, but over and above is God and faith. To walk in quiet fellowship with God. Micah, you see, talks about economic conditions. He pictures an ideal world. He tells us that Jesus Christ will come to bring that world, and then he gives us a very homely state-ment, that our minds and our wills unite. "What doth the Lord require of thee" to do good? Well, this is it: to do justly, love mercy, and walk humbly with thy God.

I rather think that George Adam Smith had something when he said that is the greatest verse in the Old Testament.

www.ingramcontent.com/pod-product-compliance
Lightning Source LLC
Chambersburg PA
CBHW031436160426
43195CB00010BB/751